1988

SILVER BURDETT SCIENCE

Centennial Edition

GEORGE G. MALLINSON
Distinguished Professor
of Science Education
Western Michigan University

JACQUELINE B. MALLINSON
Associate Professor of Science
Western Michigan University

WILLIAM L. SMALLWOOD
Head, Science Department
The Community School
Sun Valley, Idaho

CATHERINE VALENTINO
Former Director of Instruction
North Kingstown School Department
North Kingstown, Rhode Island

SILVER BURDETT COMPANY
MORRISTOWN, NJ
Atlanta, GA • Cincinnati, OH • Dallas, TX • Northfield, IL •
San Carlos, CA • Agincourt, Ontario

SILVER BURDETT
SCIENCE

Centennial Edition

GEORGE G. MALLINSON

JACQUELINE B. MALLINSON

WILLIAM L. SMALLWOOD

CATHERINE VALENTINO

THE SILVER BURDETT ELEMENTARY SCIENCE PROGRAM
1-6 PUPILS' BOOKS
AND
TEACHERS' EDITIONS LEVELS K-6

ISBN 0-382-13105-3

CONTENTS

UNIT ONE

Learning About Our Plant and Animal World

Have you ever been to a zoo? You can see many kinds of living things in a zoo. You can see lions, elephants, monkeys, and snakes. Many other kinds of living things can be seen around your home and school. You can see bees, flowers, trees, and birds. All of these living things are members of our plant and animal world.

Some members of our plant and animal world are shown here. Which of these can you name? Which can you find around your home and school? Which can you find in a zoo?

Chapter 1

Animals That Live Together

Many animals live and travel in groups. What are some words we use for groups of animals? You might think of a *school* of fish or a *pack* of wolves. If you look closely at this picture, you can see some other groups of animals. In front of the elephant you can see a *herd* of impalas. A *troop* of baboons can also be seen.

In this chapter you will learn about other groups of animals. Some of these groups are made of animals of the same kind. Other groups are made of different kinds of animals.

Waterhole in Africa

AN ANIMAL TOWN
How do prairie dogs live together?

Some animals, such as bears and tigers, spend part of their lives living alone. But many animals live in groups with other animals of their own kind. Many fish live in schools. Many deer live in herds. Many birds live in flocks. Schools, herds, and flocks are kinds of animal populations (pop yə lā′shənz). An **animal population** is a group of the same kind of animal living in an area.

White-tailed prairie dog

Black-tailed prairie dog

Another kind of animal population is a **prairie** (prãr′ē) **dog town.** Thousands of prairie dogs may live together in a single prairie dog town.

Look at the picture of the prairie dog. A prairie dog is not a dog at all. It is closely related to a squirrel. It is called a dog because of the barking sound it can make. Prairie dogs live in the grasslands of the western part of North America.

When you look at a prairie dog town, all you can see are holes. If you look at the picture on page 6, you can see why. Most of a prairie dog town is below the ground. The prairie dogs live in small "rooms" that are connected by tunnels.

mound of soil

tunnel

guard room

prairie dogs "kissing"

room with
a nest in it

Prairie dog town

There is a mound of soil around the hole at the top of a tunnel. The tunnel often leads to a room containing the nest. Along the tunnel, other rooms might be used for storing food or for sleeping. One of these rooms is called the guard room. This room is found near the top of the tunnel. When in danger, a prairie dog can move quickly into the guard room to hide.

A prairie dog town is made up of many small family groups. Each family group contains one adult male. It also contains one to four adult females and several young prairie dogs.

Prairie dogs can tell members of their family group apart from other prairie dogs. They do this by "kissing." Prairie dogs "kiss" by moving slowly toward one another while showing their teeth. They touch their front teeth together. If they do not know each other, one prairie dog will chase the other one away.

A prairie dog is just one type of animal that lives in groups. In what ways is a prairie dog town like a town of people?

Prairie dogs kissing

How can you study a local bird population?

Materials milk container / scissors / string

Procedure

A. A group of students put a bird feeder outside their classroom window. They filled the bird feeder with birdseed, bread crumbs, and sunflower seeds. Then they observed the feeder for 1 hour. They counted the different kinds of birds they saw. One of the students made a bar graph to show what they observed. Use that graph to answer these questions.

BIRDS COMING TO THE FEEDER

Number of birds / Kinds of birds

1. What kind of bird came the most to the bird feeder?
2. What kind of bird came the least to the bird feeder?
3. How many finches came to the feeder?

B. Make a simple bird feeder like the one shown. Cut out the sides of a milk carton. Run a string through the top of the carton. Hang it from a clothesline or tree branch.

C. Fill your bird feeder with birdseed, bread crumbs, bits of fruit, or sunflower seeds. Observe the feeder for 1 hour each day.

D. Make a bar graph to show the number of birds that come to your bird feeder.

Conclusion

How does using a bar graph help you to study a bird population?

INSECT COLONIES
What is life like inside an insect colony?

Like many other animals, some kinds of insects live together in groups. A group of insects that live together is called an **insect colony** (kol'ə nē). Ants and termites live in insect colonies. Insect colonies are types of animal populations.

Ant nest

Wasp nest

Honeybees and wasps are other kinds of insects that live in colonies. Honeybee colonies can be found in nests called hives. Honeybees build their hives above the ground. A hive may contain thousands of bees.

There are three types of bees in a honeybee colony. These types of bees are called the queen, the worker, and the drone (drōn). Each type of bee has a different job to do in the hive.

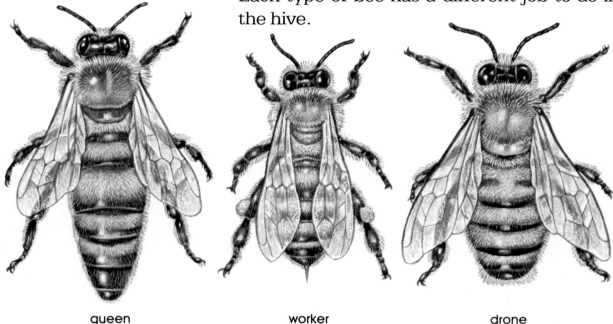

queen   worker   drone

TYPES OF HONEYBEES

Finding out

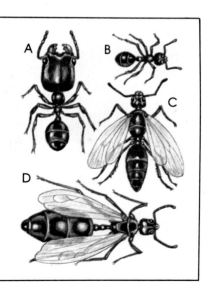

How are the ants in an ant colony different from one another?   Another kind of insect colony is an ant colony. There are different types of ants in an ant colony. Each type of ant does a different job.

You can often tell an ant's job simply by looking at it. The queen is usually the largest ant in a colony. Male ants must be able to fly to mate with the queen. Workers care for the young in the colony. Soldiers protect the colony.

Look at the harvester (här′və stər) ants shown here. What is the job of each of these ants?

The **queen** is the bee that lays all the eggs in the colony. Most of the time there is only one queen in a colony. Every colony must have a queen.

Workers are female bees that do most of the jobs in the colony. Young workers help build the hive, make and store honey, and care for the young. They also care for the queen. Older workers search for food outside the hive. Most of the bees in a colony are workers.

Drones are the only male bees in a honey-bee colony. Drones mate with the queen bee. Workers force the drones out of the hive once they are no longer needed.

Workers surrounding queen bee

Did you know that honeybees can help people? Some people set up beehives in wooden boxes. These people are called beekeepers. Beekeepers collect honey from the hives. They also collect wax made by the bees. This beeswax is used to make candles, crayons, and lipstick.

waggle dance

round dance

Do you know?

Many scientists believe that honeybees can ``tell'' each other where to find food. One way bees might do this is by doing a special dance.

When a honeybee finds food, it returns to the hive. Once in the hive, it dances in a certain pattern. If the food is nearby, the bee dances in a circle. This is called a round dance. If the food is far away, the bee dances in a figure eight. This dance is called the waggle dance.

Other worker bees watch the dance. By doing so, they can find out where the food is. The honeybee dance is one way these animals may talk to each other.

SCHOOLS OF FISH

Why do some fish swim in schools?

Fish are other animals that can live in groups. A group of the same kind of fish is called a **school.** A school is another kind of animal population. Look at the schools shown here.

Schools of fish can be found in ponds, lakes, and oceans. Some schools, like schools of tuna, may contain less than 20 fish. Others, like schools of herring, may contain millions of fish.

Hussar fish

Moorish idols

Only about one out of every five kinds of fish swims in a school. Some fish only swim in schools when they are young. Other kinds of fish live in schools all their lives. Some schools only form during the day. These schools break up at night when the fish feed. Some fish, like salmon, leave the school during mating season.

Why do fish swim in schools? One reason could be for protection. Herring are a type of fish that are protected by swimming in schools. One fish in a school of herring might swim away from something dangerous. This signals the rest of the school to swim away, too. In this way herring are safer swimming in a school than they are swimming alone.

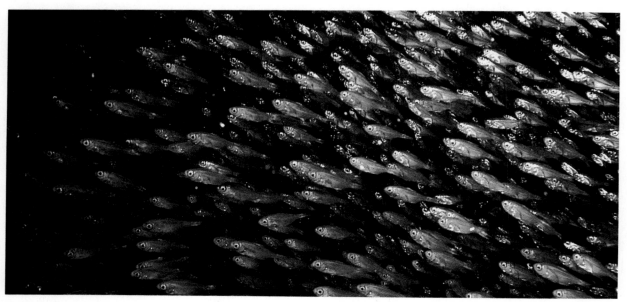

Glassy sweepers

Swimming in schools helps some fish to find food. Tuna are one example of this type of fish. Tuna swimming in a school have a better chance of finding food than does a tuna that swims alone. A school of tuna can find food in a large area easier than a single fish can.

As you can see, in some ways it is helpful for fish to swim in schools. Can you think of any way that swimming in a school could be harmful?

ANIMAL HERDS
How do animal herds differ?

Cattle

Not long ago, cowboys like this one were common throughout the West. These cowboys spent much of their time rounding up cattle. They gathered the cattle into large herds. The cowboys could move the herds great distances.

Cattle are just one kind of animal that can live in herds. Zebras, elephants, elk, and even whales also live in herds. A **herd** is another kind of animal population.

Killer whales

Elk

Burchell's zebras

African elephants

There are many kinds of animal herds. Some herds, like herds of cattle, are formed by people. Other herds, like herds of caribou (kar'ə bü), only form at certain times of the year.

Caribou can be found in parts of Alaska, northern Europe, and northern Asia. Caribou feed on small plants. In late summer these plants become harder to find. Many small groups of caribou join together to form large herds. Some of these herds are made of thousands of caribou. The herds travel to warmer places for the winter. They return the following summer when food is plentiful again.

Barren ground caribou

17

How can living in a group present a problem for animals?

Materials 16 file cards / 16 yellow crescents

Procedure

A. Your file cards stand for a population of chimpanzees. Write the word *chimp* on each of the file cards. The yellow crescents stand for bananas. The chimps will use the bananas for food.

B. Put 4 chimp cards in front of you. Divide the bananas equally between them.
   1. How many bananas does each chimp get to eat?

C. Over time, the group of chimps grows to have 8 members. Put 4 more chimp cards in front of you. Divide the bananas equally between the 8 chimps.
   2. Now how many bananas does each chimp get to eat?

D. Put the remaining 8 cards in front of you. Your group of chimps now has 16 members. Divide the bananas equally between the 16 chimps.
   3. How many bananas does each chimp get to eat now?

Conclusion

1. From what you learned here, what is one problem a large animal population might have?

2. Do you think animals share food equally? Why or why not?

— OTHER ANIMALS THAT LIVE — TOGETHER

How does a parasite affect its host?

So far you have read about animals of the same kind that live together in groups. Can you think of two different kinds of animals that live together?

Have you ever heard of insects called fleas? Some types of fleas live on dogs. Fleas suck blood from a dog's body. They depend on the dog for their food. This can be harmful to the dog. Some fleas even carry diseases that can make dogs very sick.

Living things that depend on and harm other living things are called **parasites** (par'ə-sīts). Fleas are parasites. Living things that parasites depend on are called **hosts.** A dog is a flea's host.

Springer spaniel

Female and male dog fleas

19

Some different kinds of animals live together without harming one another. Look at the fish attached to this shark. This fish is called a remora (rem'ər ə). Remoras and sharks are another example of two different animals that live together. But unlike fleas and dogs, remoras and sharks do not harm one another. Remoras eat scraps of food left by sharks. Remoras depend on sharks for this food, but they are not parasites. Remoras do not harm sharks. Some other examples of different kinds of animals that live together are shown on page 21.

Remoras on shark

Cleaner shrimp get food by removing parasites living on fish, such as this angelfish.

Birds called oxpeckers get their food by eating harmful insects that live on zebras.

A clownfish is protected by a sea anemone. In return, it attracts food for the sea anemone.

IDEAS TO REMEMBER

► A group of the same kind of animal living in an area is called an animal population.

► Prairie dogs live in prairie dog towns.

► A honeybee colony lives in a hive. A honeybee colony includes a queen, many female workers, and some drones.

► A group of the same kind of fish that swim together is called a school.

► Many deer, zebras, caribou, and elephants live in herds.

► Parasites are living things that depend on and harm other living things.

► Some different kinds of animals that live together help one another.

Reviewing the Chapter

SCIENCE WORDS

A. Use these terms to answer the questions.

animal population   parasite   drone

prairie dog town   caribou   school

insect colony   host   herd

worker   queen   herring

1. I am a living thing that a parasite depends on. What am I?
2. I am a group of the same kind of animal living in an area. What am I?
3. I am a group of the same kind of fish. What am I?
4. I am a group of insects that live together. What am I?
5. I am a group of zebras, elk, cows, or whales. What am I?
6. I am a group of the same kind of animal that lives in underground rooms that are connected by tunnels. What am I?
7. I am the bee that lays all the eggs in a honeybee colony. What am I?
8. I am a living thing that depends on and harms other living things. What am I?
9. I am a male honeybee. What am I?
10. I am one of the female bees that does most jobs in a honeybee colony. What am I?

UNDERSTANDING IDEAS

A. Copy the following groups of terms. Cross out the term that does not belong in each group. Then describe what the remaining terms have in common.

1. school, elk, pack, herd, troop
2. hive, worker, drone, soil, queen
3. tunnel, "kissing," grasslands, underground, pond
4. caribou, zebras, tuna, whales, elephants
5. honeybees, fleas, dogs, remoras, sharks

B. Identify each of these groups of animals.

1   2   3

USING IDEAS

1. A honeybee is just one type of insect that lives in a colony. Use a reference book to find out about other insects that live in colonies, such as ants or termites. Make a chart to show what jobs each member of the insect colony does.

Chapter 2

The World of Plants

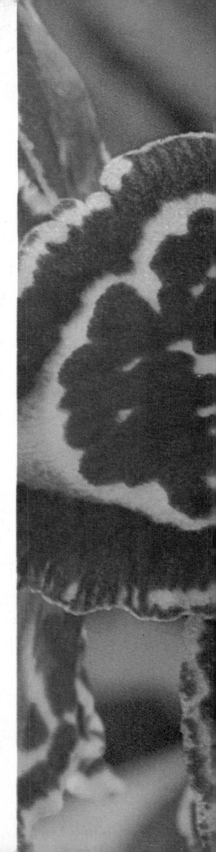

What kind of living thing is this? Is it an animal, or is it a plant? If you studied this living thing closely, you would find that it is a plant. But what kind of plant is it?

To find out, you would have to look closely at the parts of the plant. You would try to notice what makes this plant different from other plants. You can see from the picture that this plant has a colorful flower. You might also note the size and shape of the flower. Then you could look in a book to find the name of the plant. You would find that this plant is called an orchid.

In this chapter you will learn how you can tell one plant from another plant. This will help you to name different plants in the world of plants.

24

GROUPING PLANTS

What are some ways you can group plants?

Can you name any of the plants on these pages? How do you know the names? Maybe one plant has flowers you have seen before. Or maybe it has leaves that are different from other plants. There are over 350,000 kinds of plants in the world. So to name any one plant, you must tell how that plant is different from all the others.

Imagine a library that has 350,000 books. What if all the books were scattered around the library? You would have a hard time finding a certain book in such a library. To make it easier to find a certain book, librarians classify (klas′ə fī), or group, their books. Books are classified by subject in a library. Librarians put all the history books together. They do the same with other books, too.

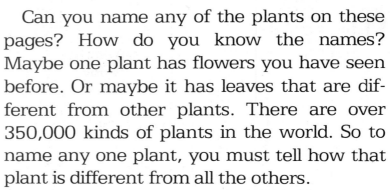

Scientists classify living things. Look at the plants on these pages. Try to classify them.

How did you classify the plants? Did you classify them by their size? By their color? Did you classify them by the shape of their leaves? Why did you classify the plants the way you did?

Some scientists classify plants by the way they reproduce (rē prə düs′), or make new plants. Some plants reproduce with seeds. Other plants do not. Scientists put all the seed plants in one group. Trees and all plants that have flowers are in this group. Scientists put all the plants that do not have seeds in a second group. This group includes ferns, mosses, fungi (fun′jī), and algae (al′jē). As you will see, classification (klas ə fə kā′shən) helps you to identify plants.

How can you identify a leaf?

U · V · W · X · Y · Z

Procedure

A. Look at the classification key shown here. Scientists use keys like this to identify plants and animals. This key will help you identify the leaves pictured here.

B. Look at leaf *U*.
   1. Describe the leaf.

C. Look at the key. Decide which statement—1a or 1b—best describes leaf *U*. Follow the directions at the end of the statement you choose. Keep reading pairs of statements and following directions until you find the name of your leaf.
   2. What is the name of leaf *U*?

D. Repeat steps **B** and **C** with the other leaves.
   3. What are the names of the other leaves?

Conclusion

How were you able to identify the leaves?

CLASSIFICATION KEY

1a If the leaf is broad and flat, go to 2a.

1b If the leaf is needle-shaped, go to 5a.

2a If the leaf is not made up of many smaller leaves, called leaflets, go to 3a.

2b If the leaf is made up of leaflets, it is a locust (lō'kəst).

3a If the leaf is more round than it is long, go to 4a.

3b If the leaf is longer than it is round, it is an oak.

4a If the leaf has pointed edges, it is a maple.

4b If the leaf is fan-shaped, it is a gingko (ging'kō).

5a If the needles are short and flat, it is a hemlock.

5b If the needles are long and thin, it is a red pine.

FLOWERING SEED PLANTS

How can you classify flowering plants?

As you can see in this classification table, seed plants make up one group of plants. The table also shows that there are two groups of seed plants. One of these groups is made up of seed plants that have cones. You will learn more about this group of seed plants in the next lesson. The second group of seed plants is made up of seed plants that have flowers. More than half of all plants are included in this group.

PLANTS

Seed Plants — Nonseed Plants

Seed plants with flowers — Seed plants with cones

monocots — dicots

When you think of a plant that has a flower, what do you think of? Do you think of a small plant that grows in a garden, like a rose or a daisy? Do you think of a plant with brightly colored parts? Well, not all flowering plants are small. In fact, many types of trees are flowering plants. And not all flowers have bright colors. Some flowers, like those on some grasses, have little color.

29

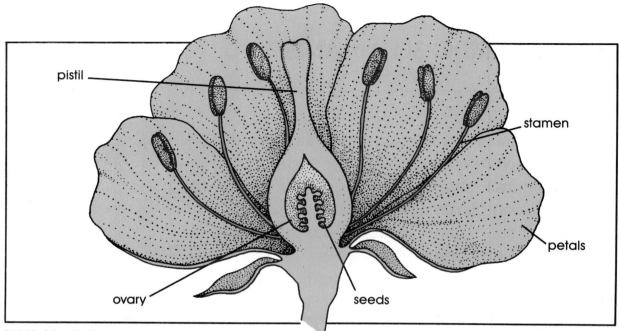

pistil

stamen

petals

ovary

seeds

PARTS OF A FLOWER

Most flowers have the same basic parts. These parts can be seen in the drawing. The petals are usually the most colorful part of the flower. Surrounded by the petals are the pistil (pis′tǝl) and the stamens (stā′mǝnz). The stamen is the male part of the flower. The pistil is the female part. The pistil and stamens are the parts of the flower that produce seeds. The seeds develop inside the base of the pistil. This part is called the ovary (o′vǝr ē).

Flowering seed plants can be divided into two groups. One group is made up of plants called monocots (mon′ǝ kots). **Monocots** are plants whose seeds have one section. The second group is made up of plants called dicots (dī′kots). **Dicots** are plants whose seeds have two sections.

30

Have you ever eaten a peanut? The part of a peanut that you eat is a seed. As you can see in the picture, a peanut splits into two sections. So a peanut plant is a dicot.

Have you ever eaten corn? A single piece of corn is called a kernel (ker'nəl). A kernel is a seed. A kernel does not have two parts. So a corn plant is a monocot.

Look at these seeds. Which seeds come from plants that are monocots? Which seeds come from plants that are dicots? How can you tell?

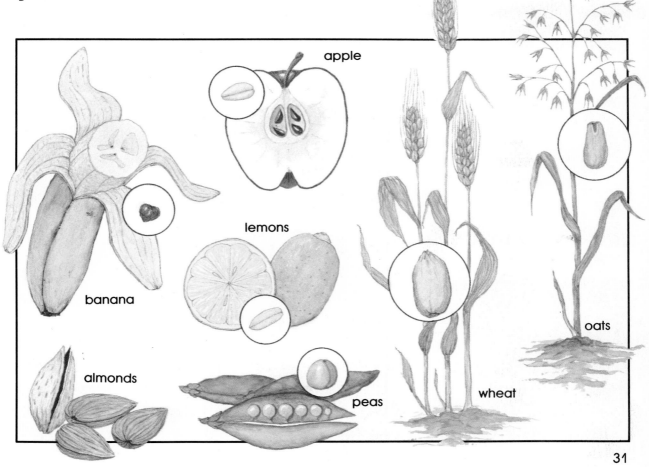

apple

banana

lemons

oats

almonds

peas

wheat

Daffodil

Yellow daisy

Looking at seeds is just one way you can classify monocots and dicots. Another way is by counting flower petals. Monocots have petals in groups of three. Dicots have petals in groups of four or five.

Count the number of petals on this daffodil (daf'ə dil). It has six petals. Six is two groups of three. So a daffodil is a monocot. Count the petals on this yellow daisy. It has eight petals. Eight is two groups of four. So a daisy is a dicot.

Now look at the other plants. How many petals does each of the flowers have? Which of these plants are monocots? Which are dicots? How can you tell?

Day lilies

Violets

Trillium

Wrinkled rose

— CONE-BEARING SEED PLANTS —
How can you identify cone-bearing plants?

Look at the classification table now. It shows some of the many types of seed plants that have cones. These plants include pines, firs, hemlocks, spruces, cedars (sē′dərs), and larches. These plants are often called **conifers** (kō′nə fərs).

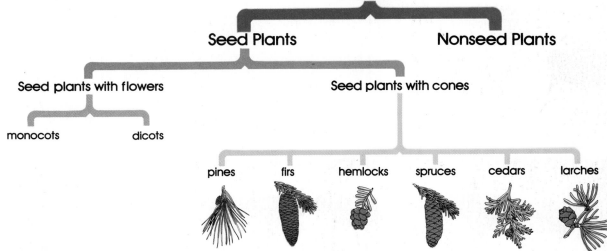

Conifers are like flowering plants in that they both use seeds to reproduce. However, conifers are different from flowering plants in several ways. For one thing, flowering plants produce seeds in flowers, while conifers produce seeds in cones. The seeds of flowering plants are protected by an ovary. The seeds of conifers are protected by the scales of the cone. Most flowering plants have broad leaves. Conifers either have needle-shaped leaves or scalelike leaves.

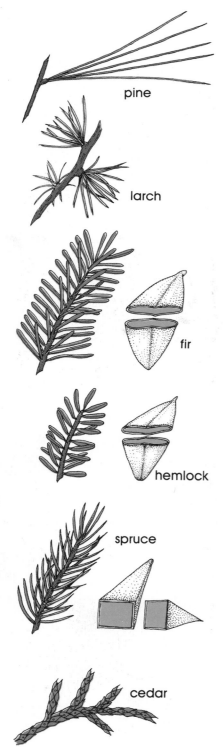

pine

larch

fir

hemlock

spruce

cedar

One way you can classify conifers is by looking at their needles. Only pines and larches have needles that grow in clusters, or groups. A larch loses its needles each autumn, while a pine does not. Firs and hemlocks have flat needles. Hemlock needles are usually shorter than fir needles. Spruces have needles that have four sides. Cedars have scalelike needles.

Look at these needles. Which of them came from a white cedar tree? Which came from an eastern hemlock? Which came from a white pine? Which came from a blue spruce? How did you identify each plant?

Do you know?

The cones of most conifers are brown and scaly. But the cones of some conifers don't look like cones at all. They look more like berries. One conifer that has this type of cone is the juniper (jü'nə pər).

Junipers can be found throughout North America. Some types of junipers are trees, while other types are shrubs. The oils that junipers produce are very useful. They are used to make some medicines and perfumes.

swamp pine

red pine

jack pine

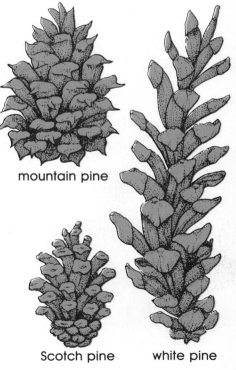

mountain pine

Scotch pine   white pine

Let's say that you have identified a tree as being a pine tree. How can you tell what kind of pine tree it is? One way is by studying the cones of the tree.

Look at these cones. They all come from different types of pine trees. As you can see, the cones are different from one another. Describe each pine cone. How is each cone different from the other pine cones?

NONSEED PLANTS

What are four types of nonseed plants?

As you can see in this classification table, there are many groups of nonseed plants. One of these groups is made up of plants that have roots, stems, and leaves. Plants in this group do not have flowers. **Ferns** make up this group.

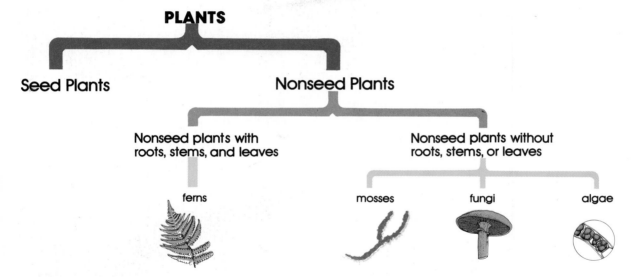

Since they do not have seeds, how do ferns reproduce? Like other nonseed plants, ferns reproduce with **spores.** These spores can be found on the underside of the leaves at certain times of the year. As you can see in the picture, these spores look like dark spots. Since ferns have leaves like seed plants, these spots can be used to help tell ferns from seed plants.

Wood ferns with spores

Moss spore pods

Ground moss

Carpet of moss

A second group of nonseed plants consists of plants that do not have true roots, stems, or leaves. This group includes **mosses, fungi,** and **algae.** These plants are sometimes called lower plants.

Mosses can be found in many damp places around the world. They grow on rocks, on trees, and in the soil. Like ferns, mosses use spores to reproduce. But unlike the spores on ferns, spores in mosses form in special structures called pods. You can see some pods in the moss shown here.

Look at these different types of mosses. How are these mosses different from ferns? How are they different from one another? How are they alike?

How can you study nonseed plants? You can set up a terrarium (tə rãr′ē əm) to further study nonseed plants. Simply get a fish tank or a large jar. Collect some mosses and ferns from damp wooded areas. Cover the bottom of the container with soil. Make the soil deep enough to plant your plants. Plant the smaller plants in the front of the container and the larger plants in the back. Water the plants. Use a reference book to identify the plants. Write the name of each plant on a small card. Set each card at the base of its plant. Seal the top of the container with plastic wrap. Keep a record of the plants' growth by marking the side of the glass with a crayon. Check the ferns for spores and the mosses for spore pods once a week.

Mold on orange

Slime mold

A second group of lower plants consists of fungi. Fungi are different from all other plants because fungi cannot make their own food. Fungi must get their food from living or dead plants and animals.

There are many types of fungi. One type is called a slime mold. Slime molds have no definite shape. They are able to move from one place to another. Yeasts are fungi that are too small to be seen without a microscope. Fungi called rusts, smuts, and rots grow on other plants and harm them. Molds that grow on food are still other types of fungi.

You might be most familiar with fungi called mushrooms. There are many kinds of mushrooms. Several kinds are shown here. How are these kinds of mushrooms different from each other?

Shaggymane mushroom

Flycap mushroom

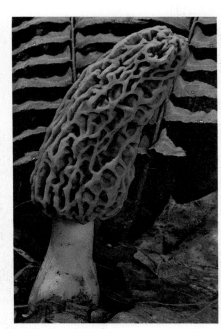

Intricate morel

39

Do preservatives stop bread mold from growing?

Materials   2 jars with lids / water / ½ slice of bread with preservatives in it / ½ slice of bread without preservatives in it / paper / crayon / hand lens / tape

Procedure

A. Sprinkle a few drops of water on a half slice of bread that has preservatives (pri zër′və tivz) in it. Put the slice in a jar. Label the jar *Preserved.* Repeat this with a half slice of bread that does not have preservatives in it. Label this jar *Not preserved.*

B. Cover and store both jars in a dark place.

C. Make a chart like the one shown here.

D. Examine both slices of bread after 3 days. Make a drawing in the chart that shows what the mold on each slice looks like.
  1. What does the mold look like?

E. Study the mold with a hand lens.
  2. What does the mold look like now?

F. Return the jars to the dark place.

G. Repeat steps **D** and **E** after 4 more days.
  3. What does the mold look like now?
  4. How has each slice of bread changed?

PICTURES OF BREAD MOLDS		
Type of bread	After 3 days	After 7 days
Bread with preservatives		
Bread without preservatives		

Conclusion

1. What differences did you notice between the bread with preservatives in it and the bread without preservatives in it?

2. Why do you think baking companies add preservatives to their breads?

A third group of lower plants consists of algae. Algae are the simplest of all food-producing plants. Algae can be grouped by color.

One type of algae is made up of blue-green algae. Blue-green algae can only be seen under a microscope. They grow in both fresh water and in salt water.

Green algae are a second type of algae. There are many types of green algae. Some types grow to lengths of 1 meter (mē′tər). Other types can only be seen with a microscope. The green scum that grows on the surface of a pond is a type of green algae.

Red algae and brown algae are two other types of algae. Most types of red algae and brown algae are found in salt water. Plants that people call seaweed are often one of these types of algae. Some types of brown algae can grow to lengths of 600 meters.

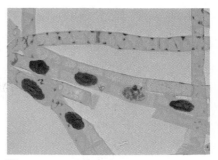
Blue-green algae

Green algae

Brown algae (kelp)

Red algae

41

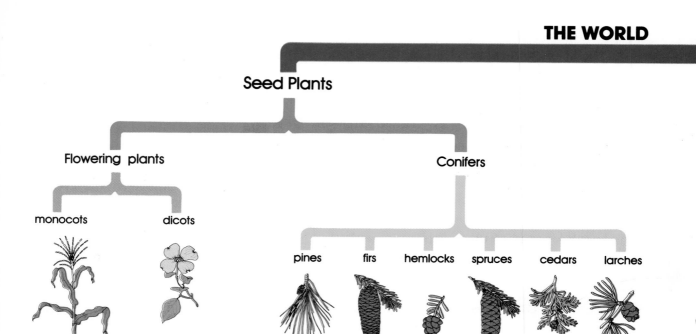

Seed Plants

Flowering plants | Conifers

monocots | dicots | pines | firs | hemlocks | spruces | cedars | larches

In this chapter you have learned about one way that scientists classify plants. You have learned how seed plants are different from nonseed plants. As you learned about different plants, you saw several sections of a classification table.

Look at the completed classification table. It shows how all plants are grouped. How are conifers and flowering plants similar? How are algae and mosses similar? How are monocots different from fungi? How are algae different from ferns?

OF PLANTS

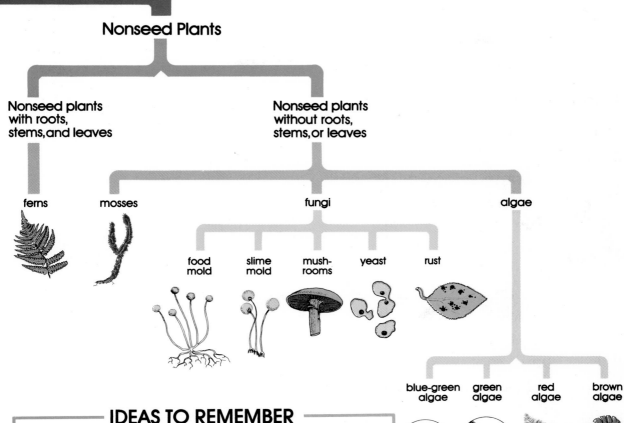

Nonseed Plants

Nonseed plants with roots, stems, and leaves

Nonseed plants without roots, stems, or leaves

ferns

mosses

fungi

food mold

slime mold

mush-rooms

yeast

rust

algae

blue-green algae

green algae

red algae

brown algae

IDEAS TO REMEMBER

▶ Two groups of plants are those that use seeds to reproduce and those that do not.

▶ Two groups of seed plants are those that have flowers and those that have cones. Two groups of flowering plants are monocots and dicots.

▶ Ferns, mosses, fungi, and algae are nonseed plants.

Reviewing the Chapter

SCIENCE WORDS

A. Use all the terms below to complete the sentences.

monocots	mosses	algae	conifers
ferns	fungi	dicots	reproduce

Some scientists classify plants by the way they __1__. Some plants use seeds while other plants do not. There are two groups of seed plants—flowering plants and __2__. Flowering plants can be divided into two groups. The __3__ are plants whose seeds have one section. Flowering plants whose seeds have two sections are called __4__. Nonseed plants that have roots, stems, and leaves are called __5__. Nonseed plants that do not have true roots, stems, or leaves include __6__, __7__, and __8__.

B. Copy the sentences below. Use science terms from the chapter to complete the sentences.

1. Ferns use ____ to reproduce.
2. Plants called ____ cannot make their own food.
3. Cone-bearing plants, such as pines, firs, and hemlocks, are often called ____.
4. In mosses, spores form in special structures called ____.
5. Plants whose seeds have one section and whose petals come in groups of three are called ____.

UNDERSTANDING IDEAS

A. Make a chart like the one shown. Give four examples of plants found in each plant group.

Plant group	Examples of plants
fungi	
conifers	
algae	
flowering plants	

B. In complete sentences, tell how conifers are similar to flowering plants and how they are different.

C. Tell whether each of the following is a monocot or a dicot.

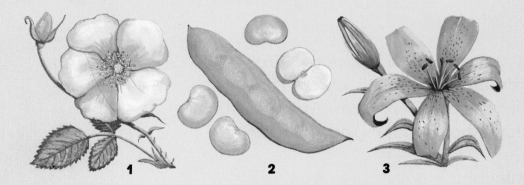

USING IDEAS

1. Look around your town for different kinds of plants. Keep a record of the plants you find. Include the date and place where you find each plant, as well as a sketch of the plant. You may want to use reference books to help you identify some of the plants.

Chapter 3

Food Chains and Food Webs

Have you ever seen a hummingbird? Hummingbirds are very small birds. They can move their wings very fast. At times they fly quickly. At other times they hover in the air.

This hummingbird is hovering in front of a flower. Hummingbirds are often found near flowers. What do hummingbirds get from flowers? What do flowers get from hummingbirds? In this chapter you will learn how living things depend on other living things for food.

light from the sun

air

food
made
in leaves

water from the roots

—LIVING THINGS NEED ENERGY —
Where do plants and animals get their energy?

Have you ever tried to work or play when you have not had enough to eat? You get tired easily when you have not eaten enough food. You need food to give you energy.

All living things need energy. Living things need energy to move and grow. Living things die if they do not get enough energy.

Where do green plants get their energy? Like other living things, green plants get energy from food. But green plants are different from other living things. Green plants can produce, or make, their own food. Green plants use sunlight, water, and air to produce food in their leaves. Plants store some of this food in their roots, stems, and leaves. Because plants produce their own food, they are often called **producers** (prə dü′sərz).

HOW PLANTS MAKE FOOD

Deer mouse

Where do animals get their energy? All animals must consume, or eat, food to get energy. Since animals consume food, they are often called **consumers** (kən sü'mərz). Some animals, like this mouse, eat green plants. These animals get energy right from the green plants. Some animals, like this hawk, eat other animals. They get energy from the animals they eat. But what if a hawk eats a mouse? The mouse got *its* energy from green plants. By eating a mouse, a hawk gets energy that once came from green plants. In fact, all animals depend on energy that comes from green plants.

Sparrow hawk

Holstein cow

Bull elk

— ANIMALS AND THEIR FOOD —
What are herbivores, carnivores, and omnivores?

At the beginning of this chapter, you read about a hummingbird. Hummingbirds eat sweet liquids made by flowers. You also read about a hawk that eats mice. Mice eat seeds and insects. As you can see, different animals eat different kinds of food. Some animals eat only plants. Some animals eat only other animals. Still other animals eat both plants and animals.

An animal that eats only plants is called a **herbivore** (hėr′bə vôr). Herbivores may eat roots, leaves, stems, fruits, flowers, or seeds. Deer, rabbits, elephants, cows, and many insects are herbivores. So are elk, squirrels, bison, and prairie dogs. Some herbivores are shown in these pictures. What kind of plant is each herbivore eating?

Eastern chipmunk

Monarch butterfly

Cheetah

Short-tailed weasel

Bobcat

Eagle owl

Some animals only eat other animals. An animal that only eats other animals is called a **carnivore** (kär′nə vôr). A wolf is a carnivore. A wolf eats rabbits, mice, and deer. Most sharks are also carnivores. These sharks eat fish. A weasel is a carnivore that eats mice. Anteaters, snakes, and owls are also carnivores. Look at the pictures of the carnivores. What kind of animal is each of these carnivores eating?

Do you know?

Animals that eat other animals are called carnivores. Some carnivores can also be called predators (pred'ə tərz). A predator is an animal that hunts other animals for food. The animal that a predator hunts is called a prey (prā). This puffin is a predator. The fish the puffin is holding is the prey. Which of the animals in the pictures on page 51 are predators? Which are the prey?

Pumpkinseed

Bear

Some animals eat both plants and other animals. These animals are called **omnivores** (om'nə vôrz). A bear is a good example of an omnivore. Bears eat berries and other fruits.

Bears also catch and eat small animals, such as fish. Some types of mice are also omnivores. So are some types of fish, birds, and turtles. Some omnivores are shown on these pages.

Eastern box turtle

Finding out

What kinds of animals live outside your home and school? Look carefully outside your home and school for some animals. Make a list of all the animals you see. Use a reference book to find out what each animal eats. Label each of the animals in your list as either a herbivore, a carnivore, or an omnivore.

FOOD CHAINS

How does a food chain show how energy moves from one living thing to another?

So far you have learned that living things need food for energy. You have also learned that green plants use energy from sunlight to make food energy. The plants store this food energy in their roots, stems, and leaves.

Do you know how energy stored in plants is used by animals? Imagine a grasshopper landing on a blade of grass. The grasshopper munches on the grass. By eating the grass, the grasshopper takes in and stores energy that was stored in the grass. After a while, a green frog spots the grasshopper. Suddenly the frog grabs and eats the insect. In doing so, the frog takes in and stores energy from the grasshopper. Later, as the green frog floats in a nearby pond, it is spotted by a smallmouth bass. In one quick motion the bass swallows the frog. The fish takes in and stores energy from the frog.

red-tailed hawk

bull snake

deer mouse

seeds

As you can see, energy from plants follows a path from one living thing to another. A path like this is called a food chain. A **food chain** is the path by which energy passes from one living thing to another.

A food chain begins with a green plant, a producer. It continues with an animal that eats the green plant, a consumer. This consumer is often a herbivore. A food chain may include one or more other consumers. These consumers may be carnivores or omnivores.

One simple food chain is made of seeds, mice, snakes, and hawks. This food chain is shown in the drawing. The arrows in the drawing point to the living things that are being eaten. In this food chain a deer mouse eats seeds. Bull snakes eat deer mice. Red-tailed hawks eat bull snakes. As you can see, this food chain leads from seeds to mice, to snakes, to hawks.

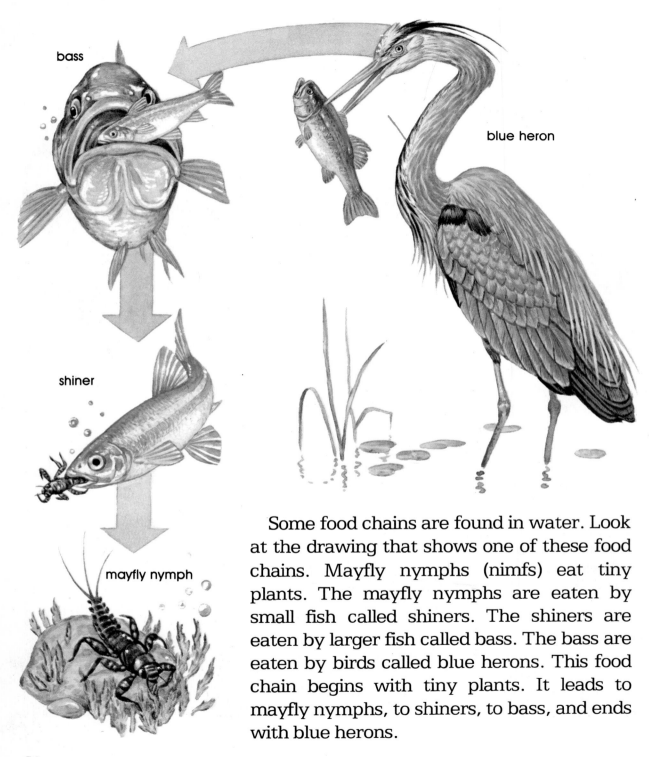

bass

blue heron

shiner

mayfly nymph

Some food chains are found in water. Look at the drawing that shows one of these food chains. Mayfly nymphs (nimfs) eat tiny plants. The mayfly nymphs are eaten by small fish called shiners. The shiners are eaten by larger fish called bass. The bass are eaten by birds called blue herons. This food chain begins with tiny plants. It leads to mayfly nymphs, to shiners, to bass, and ends with blue herons.

How do food-chain members affect each other?

Materials 2 sheets of drawing paper / scissors / glue

Procedure

A. Draw a large triangle, a rectangle, a circle, and a square on a sheet of drawing paper. All four shapes should fit on one sheet. Cut out each shape. Write the word *carnivore* on the triangle. Write the word *herbivore* on the square. Write the word *producer* on the circle. Write the words *large carnivore* on the rectangle.

B. Place the four paper shapes on a sheet of drawing paper in an order that forms a food chain. Draw arrows to show what each of the members eats.

C. Pretend that a disease has killed the herbivores in your chain. Remove the square.
　1. What happens to the carnivores in the food chain?
　2. How are the producers affected by this change?

D. Look back in this chapter and find plants and animals that might fit this chain. Label each cut-out with an animal's name. Glue each shape to your paper to show a food chain.

Conclusion

1. How do the members of a food chain depend on each other?

2. What happens to the food chain when any one member is removed?

57

FOOD WEBS

How does a food web show how all the animals in a community get energy?

You do not eat just one type of food every day. In a single day you might eat bread, fruit, and meat. In a similar way most animals eat more than one type of food. For example, you have learned that hawks eat snakes. Hawks also eat mice and rabbits. A mouse might eat seeds, nuts, and insects. A rabbit might eat many different kinds of plants.

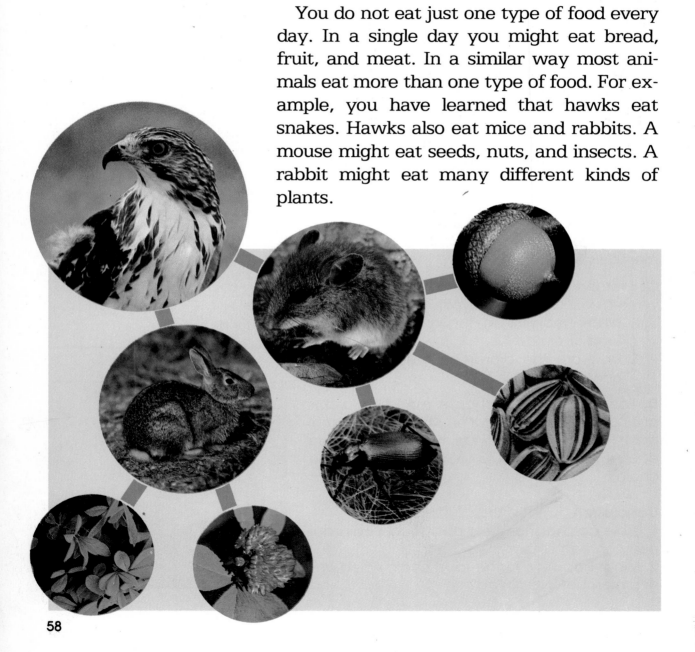

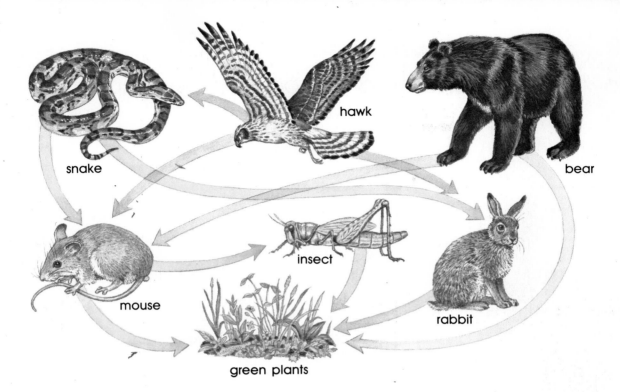

snake

hawk

bear

mouse

insect

rabbit

green plants

As you know, plants and animals live close to one another. All the plants and animals in an area make up a **community** (kə myü′nə-tē). A **food web** shows how all the animals in a community get their energy.

A food web can be thought of as being like a spider web. All the threads of a spider web are connected to each other. All the living things in a food web are also connected to each other.

Study the drawing of the food web. Look at the hawk. As you can see, hawks eat snakes, mice, and rabbits in this food web. Look at the mouse. Mice eat insects and green plants in this food web. What do bears eat in this food web?

How do the members of a food web depend on each other?

Materials   food-web card / yarn

Procedure

A. Hang a food-web card around your neck. Your food-web card shows a food chain. It tells you which member of the food chain you stand for.

   1. Which member of the food chain are you?

B. Find the other members of your food chain. Connect your food chain by having everyone in your group hold on to a long piece of yarn together.

   2. What are the other members of your food chain?

C. Keep your food chain connected with the piece of yarn. Then find other food chains that have been formed by your classmates. Look for a member of another food chain that you can feed on. With your free hand, hold a new piece of yarn between you and this other member.

   3. What did you form?

D. Pretend that a flood has destroyed the producers in your food web. All producers should let go of their yarn and sit down.

   4. What do you think might happen to the other members of your food web?

Conclusion

1. How does every member of a food web depend on producers?

2. What happens to the other members of a food web when one group of members dies off?

IDEAS TO REMEMBER

▶ Living things need energy to live. They get energy from food.

▶ An animal that eats only plants is called a herbivore.

▶ An animal that eats other animals is called a carnivore.

▶ An animal that eats both plants and animals is called an omnivore.

▶ A food chain shows how energy passes from one living thing to another.

▶ A food web shows how all the animals in a community get energy.

Reviewing the Chapter

SCIENCE WORDS

A. Write the letter of the term that best matches the definition. Not all the terms will be used.

1. An animal that eats only plants
2. An animal that a predator hunts
3. A green plant
4. An animal that eats both plants and animals
5. Something that shows how all the animals in a community get their energy
6. Something that is needed by all living things
7. An animal that eats only other animals
8. An animal that hunts other animals for food
9. The path by which energy passes from one living thing to another
10. All the plants and animals in an area

a. predator
b. food chain
c. consumer
d. prey
e. community
f. herbivore
g. energy
h. producer
i. food web
j. carnivore
k. omnivore

UNDERSTANDING IDEAS

A. Show a food chain made up of each of the following groups.

    1. lettuce, rabbit, wolf
    2. grasshopper, frog, grass, bass
    3. mouse, sunflower seed, weasel

B. Copy the following groups of living things. All but one living thing in each group get their energy in the same way. Cross out this one living thing in each group. Describe what the remaining living things have in common.

    1. apple tree, mouse, clover, grass
    2. deer, wolf, rabbit, squirrel
    3. wolf, anteater, elk, hawk
    4. bear, turtle, weasel

C. Look at the picture of the food web on page 59. Write down three food chains that you can see in the picture. Explain what is happening in each food chain.

USING IDEAS

1. Venus's-flytraps and pitcher plants are two plants that eat insects. Use a reference book to find out about these unusual plants. How do they capture their food? How do they get energy from the food once they have captured it?

Chapter 4

How Living Things Survive

Have you ever tried to hold a live fish? A live fish flips back and forth. It is very slippery and hard to hold. Yet an osprey can easily catch and hold a live fish. The osprey has sharp claws to grasp the body of the fish.

This osprey may be taking the fish to its nest. Ospreys build their nests in tall trees or on high rocky ledges. They have large wings to help them carry food to these places.

Ospreys have sharp claws and large wings that help them survive. In this chapter you will learn about body parts and activities that help other living things survive.

Leopard

Dolphin

— WHY LIVING THINGS ARE — DIFFERENT

What things help living things to survive?

Stop and think about how living things are different from one another. Each kind of living thing has certain body parts that make it different from other kinds of living things. An eagle is covered with feathers. A fish is covered with scales. Pine trees have cones, while apple trees have flowers. Living things also have their own way of doing certain things. Robins build their nests out of twigs. Honeybees build part of their hives out of beeswax. How are the living things in the pictures different from one another?

Moth

Apples

Black bar soldierfish

Some of the body parts or activities of a living thing help it to survive (sər vīv′), or stay alive. A body part or an activity that helps a living thing to survive is called an **adaptation** (ad ap tā′shən). Feathers, scales, and flowers are adaptations. Activities such as building a nest are also adaptations.

Compare the feathers of the bird with the scales of the fish. How might feathers help a bird to survive? How might scales help a fish to survive? Could a fish survive with feathers? Could a bird survive with scales?

Blue jay

TREES CHANGE WITH THE SEASONS

Why do some trees change each season?

Have you ever noticed how some trees change during the year? A maple tree is one kind of tree that changes with each season. A maple tree is bare during the winter. But if you look closely, you can find tiny buds on the tree. These buds begin to grow in the spring. They slowly open up to become broad green leaves. During the summer a maple tree is covered with green leaves. Late in the summer some of the green leaves turn bright red or orange. By autumn the whole tree is covered with brightly colored leaves. As winter approaches, all the leaves fall off the tree.

Norway maple—winter

Norway maple—spring

The changes that take place in a maple tree are a type of adaptation. How do these changes help the tree to survive? Maple trees are like most other types of green plants. Maple trees take in water from the ground through their roots. They lose water through their leaves.

If maple trees kept their leaves during the winter, they would lose water through their leaves. But in most places where maple trees grow, water in the ground freezes during the winter. So the maple trees would not be able to replace the water they lost. Without water, the trees would soon die.

By losing their leaves during the winter, maple trees do not lose much water. This helps them to survive the winter. So the act of losing leaves is an adaptation.

Norway maple—summer

Norway maple—autumn

If maple trees must lose their leaves to survive the winter, then why do pine trees keep most of their needles? Needles are actually long thin leaves. But needles are different from the broad leaves found on maple trees. Trees that have needles lose very little water through their needles. So pine trees do not have to lose all of their needles to survive during the winter. Since needles help pine trees to survive, they are an adaptation of pine trees. What are some other adaptations of pine trees?

Ponderosa pines—winter

Ponderosa pines—summer

PLANT ADAPTATIONS

What adaptations help plants to get sunlight and water?

Green plants need certain things to survive. One of these things is sunlight. Green plants grow toward light. But many times tall plants, such as trees, keep sunlight from reaching smaller plants. These smaller plants must have adaptations to help them get the sunlight they need.

Some small plants are able to climb to get sunlight. Different plants climb in different ways. Bean plants can climb by twisting their stems around larger plants. Rose plants can climb by hooking their thorns into larger plants. Ivy uses special roots to climb buildings. Cucumbers and peas can use structures called tendrils (ten'drəls) to climb larger plants. **Tendrils** are thin coiled structures that help plants to climb. Which of these climbing adaptations do you think is the best? Why?

Ivy

Pole bean

Grape tendril

Another way small plants can get the sunlight they need is by growing on other plants. Plants that grow on other plants are common in jungles. Orchids (ôr′kids) and Spanish moss are two plants that have this adaptation. Spanish moss grows in many places in the southern United States. What problems might this adaptation cause?

Spanish moss

Orchids

Finding out

How does sunlight affect plants? Place a small potted plant on a windowsill. Give the plant water when it needs it. After a few days you will notice that all the leaves face the window. Turn the pot around so that the leaves face inside. Wait a few more days. What happened? How might this adaptation help plants to survive?

A second thing plants need to survive is water. Getting water is not a problem for most plants. But it is a big problem for plants that grow in deserts.

A creosote (krē′ə sōt) bush is a desert plant that gives off chemicals from its roots. These chemicals kill any plants growing nearby. The creosote bush can then get water that would have been taken by the other plants.

Cactus plants have adaptations that help them to get and to store water. The roots of cactus plants cover a large area. They do not grow very deep into the ground. This helps cactus plants to take in as much water as possible when it rains.

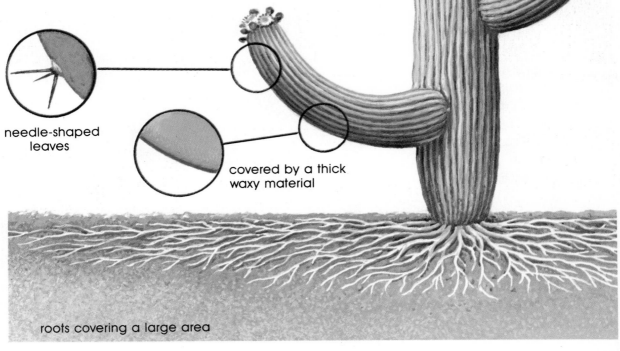

needle-shaped
leaves

covered by a thick
waxy material

roots covering a large area

ADAPTATIONS THAT HELP CACTUS PLANTS GET AND SAVE WATER

Prickly pear cactus

Cactus plants are able to store large amounts of water in their stems. They do not lose much water from their stems or leaves. Their stems are covered with a thick waxy material. Their "leaves" are spines. Like pine trees with their needles, cactus plants lose very little water through their spines. Why don't cactus plants lose their spines each autumn as maple trees lose their leaves?

Do you know?

Many plants have adaptations that help to keep them from being eaten by animals. Some plants, like cactus plants, are covered with sharp spines. Other plants, like a honey locust tree, are covered with thorns. Still other plants contain chemicals that harm animals. Poison ivy, shown here, is one of these plants. How does poison ivy affect people?

ANIMAL ADAPTATIONS

What adaptations help animals get food?

Compare this zebra and giraffe. Zebras and giraffes are often found in the same places. Both zebras and giraffes eat plants. How are zebras and giraffes different? For one thing, giraffes have a much longer neck than zebras do. But if they live in the same places and eat the same things, why do zebras and giraffes look so different?

Giraffes

Burchell's zebra

Like plants, animals have adaptations that make them look different from other animals. And like plant adaptations, animal adaptations help animals to get what they need to survive. A giraffe uses its long neck to reach leaves on trees. A zebra uses its shorter neck to reach grasses.

Pileated woodpecker

Most animals have adaptations that help them to get food. Look at the birds shown here. Each of these birds has a different type of beak. Each kind of beak is an adaptation that helps the bird to get a certain kind of food.

Song sparrow

Little blue heron

Brown pelican

Calliope hummingbird

King vulture

Sparrows (spar'ōs) have short thick beaks that they use to crush seeds. Hummingbirds have long thin beaks that are used to get food that is deep within a flower. Eagles and vultures (vul'chərs) use their hooked beaks to tear meat. Woodpeckers use their long hard beaks to peck into wood to look for insects. Both pelicans (pel'ə kəns) and herons (her'əns) feed on fish. Compare their beaks. A heron spears fish, while a pelican scoops fish.

Rose-breasted grosbeak

Look at the beaks of the grosbeak (grōs′bēk), the duck, and the tern in the pictures. Which of these birds spears fish? Which bird feeds on seeds? Which bird eats plant materials floating in water? For what reasons did you make each choice?

Ruddy duck

Common tern

Do you know?

Many insects have adaptations that help to keep them from being eaten by other animals. For example, some insects look like other living things. A walking stick is an insect that looks like a stick. The leaf butterfly shown here looks like a leaf. How might this type of adaptation help an insect to survive?

How does the size of a bird's beak help it to get food?

Materials   2 clothespins / 2 long pieces of an ice-cream stick / 2 short pieces of an ice-cream stick / glue / several short pieces of a plastic straw

Procedure

A. Glue two long pieces of an ice-cream stick to a clothespin, as shown. Glue two short pieces of an ice-cream stick to another clothespin. Let the glue dry. Think of each clothespin as a bird. One bird has a long beak, while the other bird has a short beak.

B. Use the short-beaked bird to pick up a piece of a plastic straw.
   1. What did the short beak do to the straw?

C. Use the long-beaked bird to pick up another piece of straw.
   2. What did the long beak do to the straw?

D. Compare the straws being held by the beaks.
   3. Which beak put the most force on its straw?

Conclusion

1. Many seed-eating birds crack open their food. Would it be better for these birds to have a short beak or a long beak? Why?

2. Some other birds eat soft foods, like berries. What type of beak would be better for these birds to have? Why?

WINTER ADAPTATIONS OF ANIMALS

What adaptations help animals in the winter?

All animals find it hard to survive during the winter. It is often difficult for animals that eat plants to find food. Some animals can freeze to death in the cold temperatures of winter. All animals must have adaptations to help them survive the winter.

Some animals travel great distances during the winter. This adaptation is called **migration** (mī grā′shən). Whales, wildebeests, and many types of birds migrate.

Wildebeests

Canadian geese

Monarch butterflies

Animals often migrate in large groups. Elk migrate in large herds, which may have thousands of animals. Millions of monarch butterflies migrate together.

Arctic tern

Different kinds of animals migrate different distances. Robins migrate only as far south as is needed to find food. Other birds, called terns, migrate from the North Pole to the South Pole. This trip is about 35,000 km.

How are some animals adapted to travel in snow?

Cottontail rabbit

Varying hare

Materials animal tracks / graph paper / scissors

Procedure

A. From your teacher, get a sheet of paper with the tracks of a varying (vãr'ē ing) hare and a cottontail rabbit on it. A varying hare is about the same size as a cottontail rabbit.

B. Cut out the varying hare tracks. Trace the outline of the tracks on a sheet of graph paper. Count the number of squares that the tracks cover on the graph paper.
   1. About how many squares do the varying hare tracks cover?

C. Repeat step **B** with the cottontail rabbit tracks.
   2. About how many squares do the cottontail rabbit tracks cover?
   3. Which animal's feet cover a larger area?

Conclusion

1. Some people wear snowshoes to help them walk in deep snow. By wearing snowshoes your feet cover a larger area. This helps to keep you from sinking in the snow. Which animal has feet that would be better for traveling in deep snow—a varying hare or a cottontail rabbit?

2. Which animal would you expect to live farther north?

Some animals that do not migrate spend the winter in hibernation (hī bər nā′shən). **Hibernation** is a long, deep sleep. Squirrels, woodchucks, and chipmunks have this adaptation. Brown bats and birds called swifts also hibernate.

Animals that hibernate store food as fat in their bodies during the autumn. When the weather turns cold, they crawl into a safe place, such as a cave or a deep hole. There they fall into a deep sleep. Some animals wake up many times during the winter. Others do not wake up until spring.

Ground squirrel

IDEAS TO REMEMBER

► An adaptation is a body part or an activity that helps a living thing to survive.
► Plant adaptations help plants to survive the winter, to get sunlight, and to get and keep water.
► Most animals have adaptations that help them to get food.
► Migration and hibernation are two adaptations that help animals to survive the winter.

Reviewing the Chapter

SCIENCE WORDS

A. Write the letter of the term that best matches the definition. Not all the terms will be used.

1. A thin coiled structure that helps plants to climb
2. The movement of animals from one place to another during the winter
3. A long, deep sleep
4. A body part or an activity that helps a living thing to survive

a. adaptation
b. beak
c. tendril
d. hibernation
e. migration

UNDERSTANDING IDEAS

A. Write a sentence to tell how each animal below survives the winter.

1   2   3

B. Make a table like the one shown. Using what you learned in the chapter, fill in the empty spaces.

Type of bird	What its beak looks like	What its beak is used for
sparrow	short and thick	
	long and thin	get food from deep within flower
eagle	hooked	
woodpecker		peck into wood to get insects
pelican		scoops fish
	long and pointed	spears fish

C. Explain how maple trees survive the winter by losing their leaves. How can pine trees survive the winter without losing all their needles?

USING IDEAS

1. A turtle has a hard shell. The fur on a snowshoe rabbit turns white during the winter. How do their adaptations help these animals to survive?

2. Make a booklet of bird pictures. Explain how the beak and feet of each bird help it to get food.

Science in Careers

People who are interested in working with living things might consider a career in conservation. Conservation is the management, protection, and wise use of natural resources. *Conservationists* are also called *ecologists.* Many careers in conservation require a person to have a college degree.

Forest fire fighter

Wildlife biologist

A person with an interest in animals might become a *wildlife biologist.* Some wildlife biologists try to determine how many animals are living in a certain area. They also try to find ways to protect the animals from being harmed by people.

People with an interest in plants often look for jobs in forestry. The U.S. Forest Service, the National Park Service, state forest agencies, and logging companies need *foresters.* Foresters study the science of growing trees, fire protection, and disease control.

People in Science

Aldo Leopold (1887–1948)

Aldo Leopold became interested in nature at an early age. He believed that people should enjoy wilderness areas as places for recreation. But he also believed that the wilderness should be preserved as much as possible. He asked the U.S. Forest Service to preserve a half-million acres of the Gila National Forest in New Mexico as an undisturbed wilderness area. People are able to enjoy this area today because of Aldo Leopold.

Gila National Forest

Developing Skills

WORD SKILLS

The Glossary and Index for this book begin on page 348. The Glossary shows you the meanings of important terms. The Key to Pronunciation at the beginning of the Glossary shows the symbols used in respelling these terms. The Index, which follows the Glossary, shows the pages on which important topics are discussed.

Use the Glossary and Index to answer these questions.

1. What term is respelled (hī-bər nā′shən)? What does this term mean?
2. On what page could you find out more about this term?
3. What term is respelled (kən-sü′mər)? What does this term mean?
4. On what page could you find out more about this term?

READING A MAP

Look at the map on the next page. It gives information about where black-tailed and white-tailed prairire dogs can be found. As you can see, black-tailed prairie dogs and white-tailed prairie dogs are usually found in different places. Use the map to answer the following questions.

1. Can white-tailed prairie dogs be found in Idaho?
2. Can black-tailed prairie dogs be found in Alberta?
3. A friend tells you that she saw a prairie dog town in North Dakota. What kind of prairie dog is it?
4. In which states and provinces can both kinds of prairie dogs be found?

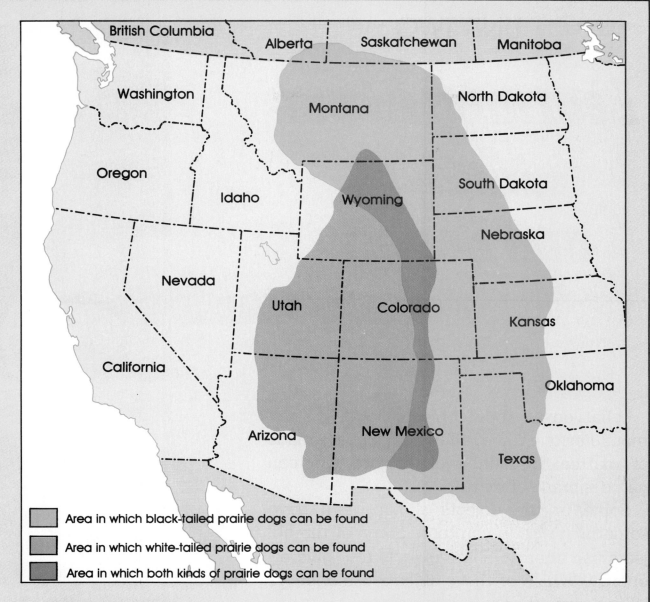

Area in which black-tailed prairie dogs can be found

Area in which white-tailed prairie dogs can be found

Area in which both kinds of prairie dogs can be found

MAKING A MAP

Trace a map of North America. Use a reference book to find out where white-tailed jackrabbits and black-tailed jackrabbits live. Use colored pencils to indicate these areas on your map. Is there any area in which both kinds of jackrabbits live?

Learning About Matter and Energy

What do all these objects have in common? For one thing, all the objects are made of matter. In fact, every object you can name is made of matter.

Some of the objects shown here have something else in common. Some of the objects use energy. Some objects also give off energy. Which of these objects use energy? Which give off energy?

In this unit you will learn about matter and energy. You will find out how matter is measured. You will also find out about different forms of energy and how energy is used by machines to do work.

Chapter 5

Measuring Matter

What would happen if the carpenters did not measure as they built this house? The floors might be slanted. The windows might not fit. The doors might not close. There could be cracks and spaces in the walls. Some of the boards might be too long.

Measuring is important in many ways. You use some kind of measurement every day. In this chapter you will learn about some things that can be measured. You will also learn how to measure them.

— THE PROPERTIES OF MATTER —
What is a property?

What kinds of things have you measured? You may have measured how tall you are. You may have measured the amount of milk to put in a recipe. You may have measured how much you weigh.

All these things that you can measure are matter. **Matter** is anything that has mass and takes up space. Water is matter, and air is matter. You are made of matter.

This picture shows different examples of matter. What makes these kinds of matter different? To answer this, you might make a list. Your list might say that the stone is hard. The ice is cold. The gold is yellow. The apple tastes sweet and the vinegar tastes sour. You could go on until you had a long list.

Each of the things on your list is a property (prop'ər tē) of matter. A **property** is something that describes matter. Color, hardness, size, shape, and taste are examples of properties.

Some properties can be measured, while others cannot. For example, you cannot measure taste, but you can measure size. In the rest of this chapter, you will learn about some of the properties of matter that can be measured.

THE LENGTH OF MATTER
How do you measure length?

The distance around this track has been measured so that the runners can race. Length is a property of matter that can be measured. **Length** is a measured distance. A metric ruler or tape measure is a tool for measuring length.

The **centimeter** (sen′tə mē tər) is a unit used to measure length. The symbol for centimeter is *cm*. The centimeter is a small unit of measurement. A pencil is about 20 cm long. Your height is probably over 120 cm.

Suppose you wanted to measure a book. First you would place the ruler on the book. The zero point of the ruler would be even with the edge of the book, as in the picture. You would then count the number of centimeters from this point to the other end of the book. If you look closely at the picture, you will see that the book measures 25 cm.

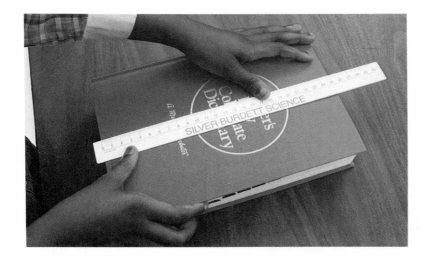

Finding out

How is a ruler used to measure length? Use a metric ruler to measure some parts of your body. Place the zero point of the ruler at the tip of your thumb. Count the number of centimeters from the tip to the base to find its length. Use a string to measure around parts such as your wrist. Then measure the string to find the length. Also measure your foot, your hand, your head, and your waist.

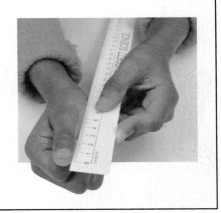

Large objects are usually measured in meters. A **meter** is a unit of length equal to 100 cm. The symbol for meter is *m*. Distances in sporting events are usually measured in meters.

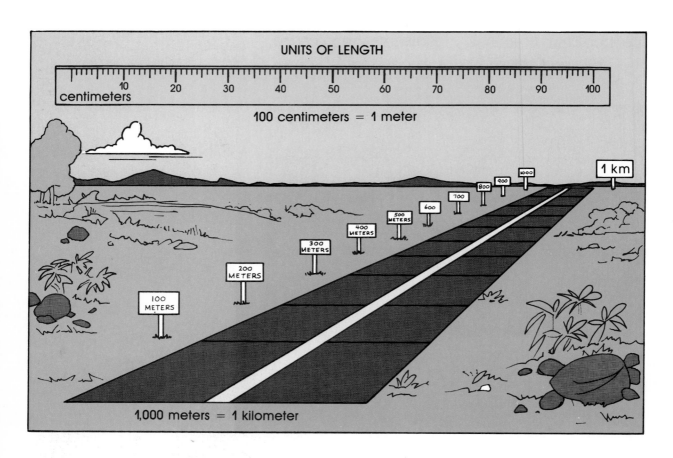

UNITS OF LENGTH

10 centimeters   20   30   40   50   60   70   80   90   100

100 centimeters = 1 meter

100 METERS   200 METERS   300 METERS   400 METERS   500 METERS   600   700   800   900   1000   1 km

1,000 meters = 1 kilometer

DEL. WATER GAP.
37 MILES
60 KILOMETERS

Very large distances are measured in kilometers (kil′ə mē tərs). A **kilometer** is a unit of length equal to 1,000 m. The symbol for kilometer is *km*. Many road signs use kilometers to give the distance between two locations. Have you ever seen a sign like this?

MASS OF MATTER

How do you measure mass?

The barbells in these pictures are made of the same kind of matter. Both are made of iron. What properties do they have that are different?

One of the first things you might notice is that one barbell is larger than the other. The large barbell is also heavier than the other. The large barbell is heavier because it contains more iron. It has greater mass than the small barbell. Mass is a property of all matter. **Mass** is the amount of matter in an object. Things that contain more matter have greater mass. Things that contain less matter have lesser mass.

Empty balance

Balance with clip and masses

These pictures show the same kind of matter—wood. Which picture shows the greatest mass? If you think the tree has the greatest mass, you are right.

Mass is a property that can be measured. A **balance,** such as the one shown in the picture, is a tool for measuring mass. A balance has two pans. If objects having the same mass are placed in each pan, they balance each other. If objects having different masses are placed in each pan, the balance tips toward the greater mass.

Suppose you wanted to use a balance to find the mass of a paper clip. As you can see, you would first put the paper clip on one pan. Next you would add mass to the other pan until the two pans balanced.

Each of the small pieces of metal in the pan has a mass of 1 gram. A **gram** is a unit of mass. The symbol for a gram is *g*. It took two of these 1-g masses to balance the paper clip. So the mass of the paper clip is 2 g.

A gram is too small to be a useful unit for measuring large masses. For example, your mass is probably more than 20,000 g. The mass of larger things is usually measured in kilograms (kil'ə grams). A **kilogram** is a unit of mass equal to 1,000 g. The symbol for kilogram is *kg*. Your mass is probably a little more than 20 kg.

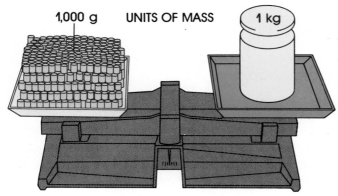

1,000 g   UNITS OF MASS   1 kg

1,000 grams = 1 kilogram

Finding out

Can you use a metric balance to measure mass?
Get a balance and some metric masses. Put a pencil on one pan of the balance. Add masses to the other pan until the two pans balance. Be sure to add one mass at a time. What is the mass of your pencil? Try to find the mass of other objects.

How is a balance used to measure mass?

Materials metric ruler / pencil / piece of cardboard, 40 cm × 4 cm / 2 small paper cups / tape / large nail / 2 large books / coin / paper clips / objects provided by your teacher

Procedure

A. Hold a metric ruler straight across a piece of cardboard and make a mark at 2 cm, 20 cm, and 38 cm.

B. Tape a paper cup at the 2 cm mark on the cardboard and another paper cup at the 38 cm mark, as shown.

C. Push a large nail through the cardboard at the 20 cm mark.

D. Make a balance by resting the nail on two large books, as shown.

E. Place a coin in one of the cups.
  1. What happens to the balance?

F. Add paper clips to the other cup, one at a time, until the cups balance. You are using a paper clip as a unit of mass.
  2. How many paper clips are needed to balance the cups?
  3. What is the mass of the coin?

G. Find the masses of other objects provided by your teacher.
  4. What do you predict the mass of each object will be?
  5. What is the mass of each object?

Conclusion

How can the balance you made measure mass?

VOLUME

How do you measure volume?

You have learned that mass is a property of all matter. This picture shows another property of matter. It shows that matter takes up space. These clothes are taking up more space than there is in the suitcase. The volume (vol'yəm) of the clothes is greater than the volume of the suitcase. The **volume** of an object is the amount of space it takes up.

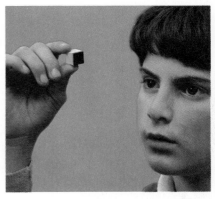

The picture shows a cube, which we will use as a unit for measuring volume. The cube is 1 cm high, 1 cm wide, and 1 cm thick. To find the volume of something, you would find out how many cubes would fill it. For example, it takes 2,400 cubes to fill this shoebox. So the volume of the box is 2,400 cubes.

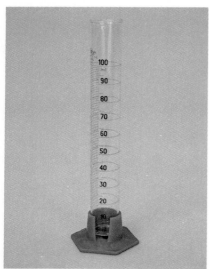

Liquids also have the property of volume. Suppose you wanted to find the volume of the water in this bottle. The bottle is not shaped like a shoebox, so you cannot measure its volume in cubes. Instead you could use a graduate (graj′ü it), like the one shown in the picture. A **graduate** is a tool used to measure the volume of liquids.

The volume of a liquid is measured in units called milliliters (mil′ə lē tərs). The symbol for milliliter is *mL*. A **milliliter** is the same amount of volume as the cube (1 cm × 1 cm × 1 cm). A tiny glass box the same size and shape as this cube would hold 1 mL of water. Liquids in small bottles are measured in milliliters.

This picture shows how to use a graduate to measure the volume of the water in the bottle. The mark on the graduate shows that the bottle holds 50 mL of water.

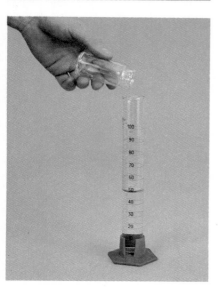

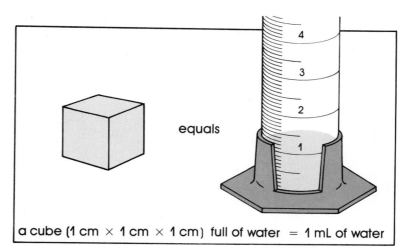

a cube (1 cm × 1 cm × 1 cm) full of water = 1 mL of water

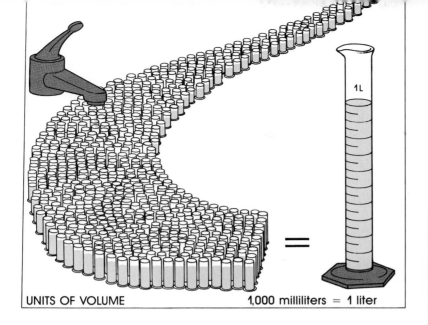

UNITS OF VOLUME   1,000 milliliters = 1 liter

Milliliters are very small units of volume. Large volumes of liquid are measured in bigger units. These units are called liters. The symbol for liter is *L*. One **liter** is equal to 1,000 mL. Juice in large jars is often measured in liters.

You can also use a graduate to measure the volume of a solid, such as a marble. Here's how. Fill a graduate with water. Drop a marble into the water. The marble takes up space that had water in it. The marble displaces (dis plās'əs), or pushes aside, the water. This is called displacement (dis-plās'mənt). You can measure the increase of water level in the graduate to find the volume of the marble. Displacement is a good way to measure the volume of odd-shaped solids. Cubes cannot be used to measure the volume of odd-shaped solids.

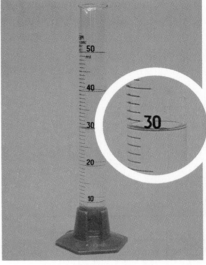

Graduate without marble

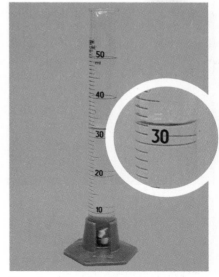

Graduate with marble

How is a graduate used to measure the volume of a rock?

Materials   graduate / water / rock

Procedure

A. Set a graduate on a table, away from the edge. Fill it to a level *below* the 20-mL mark.

B. Look closely at the surface of the water. Your eyes should be even with the water level. You will see that the surface of the water is curved.
   1. Draw the shape of the curve.

C. Add water slowly until the bottom of the curve is exactly even with the 20-mL mark.

D. Place a rock in the water. Be careful not to splash any water out.

E. Look at the water level.
   2. What is the new volume?
   3. How much did the rock increase the volume? (*Hint:* Subtract 20 mL from the volume of the water and rock together.)
   4. What is the volume of the rock?

Conclusion
1. Where did the pushed water go?
2. How much water did the rock push aside?

Using science ideas
Use your graduate to find the volume of a crayon.

DENSITY

How do you measure density?

Both pans of this balance hold objects with the same mass. One pan holds an iron nail. The other holds a piece of wood. You can see that the wood has a bigger volume than the nail. What do you think would happen if the piece of wood were the same size as the nail? If you think the balance would tip toward the nail, you are right.

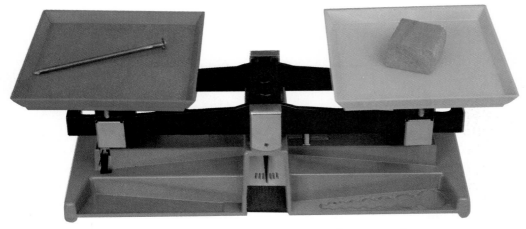

A piece of iron has more mass than a piece of wood with the same volume. Iron has a greater density (den'sə tē) than wood. Density is another property that can be measured. **Density** is the mass in a certain volume of matter. For example, the mass of one cube (1 cm × 1 cm × 1 cm) of iron is about 8 g. The mass of one cube (1 cm × 1 cm × 1 cm) of wood is less than 1 g.

You have learned that the mass of an object depends on the amount of matter it contains. Objects that have different densities have different amounts of matter in the same volume. A cube of iron contains more matter than the same sized cube of wood.

Most kinds of solid matter have greater density than most liquids. In most solids the matter is packed more tightly than in most liquids. One cube (1 cm × 1 cm × 1 cm) of iron contains more matter than one cube (1 cm × 1 cm × 1 cm) of water.

Do you know?

Can you imagine measuring without using a ruler or a scale? Long ago, people didn't have either rulers or scales. They measured the length of objects with parts of their bodies. Sometimes they used the length of a person's foot or the width of a person's hand. Mass was measured with grains of wheat or with stones. What problems do you think these types of measurements could cause?

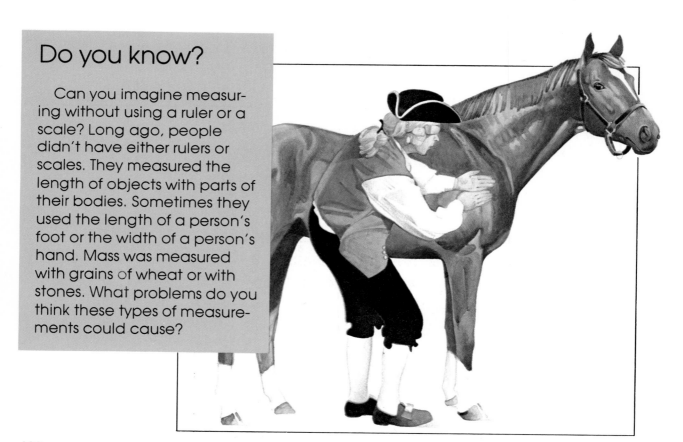

You can compare the densities of different kinds of solid matter to the densities of liquids. Solid matter sinks in a liquid if the solid has a greater density than the liquid. If the solid has a lower density than the liquid, the solid floats. These two kinds of soap have different densities. Which one has more matter in one cube than water?

You can also compare the densities of different kinds of gases. Which gas has a lower density—the helium in a balloon or the air the balloon floats in?

IDEAS TO REMEMBER

▶ Matter is anything that has mass and takes up space.

▶ Length is a measured distance. Centimeters (cm), meters (m), and kilometers (km) are units of length.

▶ Mass is the amount of matter in an object. The units used to measure mass are the gram (g) and the kilogram (kg).

▶ The volume of an object is the amount of space it takes up. The volume of liquids is measured in milliliters (mL) and liters (L).

▶ Density is the mass in a certain volume of matter.

Reviewing the Chapter

SCIENCE WORDS

A. Write the letter of the term that best matches the definition. Not all the terms will be used.

1. A unit of volume
2. A measured distance
3. A unit equal to 1,000 m
4. The amount of space an object takes up
5. A tool for measuring mass
6. Anything that has mass and takes up space
7. A unit equal to 1,000 g
8. A tool used to measure the volume of liquids
9. The amount of matter in an object
10. Something that describes matter

a. kilometer
b. property
c. milliliter
d. mass
e. graduate
f. length
g. balance
h. gram
i. volume
j. matter
k. kilogram

B. Copy the sentences below. Use science terms from the chapter to complete the sentences.

1. A unit of volume equal to 1,000 mL is a ___.
2. A ___ is a small unit that can be used to measure the length of a pencil.
3. A ___ is a unit of length equal to 100 cm.
4. The mass in a certain volume of matter is called ___.

UNDERSTANDING IDEAS

A. Choose two tools that are used to measure matter. Explain how each tool is used.

B. Make a chart like the one shown. Fill in the empty spaces using information from the chapter.

UNITS OF MEASUREMENT		
Measurement	Units	Symbol
volume		L
	meters	m
mass	grams	
	milliliters	
		kg

C. Tell which of the following sentences are true and which are false.

1. Some properties of matter can be measured.
2. All solids sink in water.
3. Air is matter.

USING IDEAS

1. Make a list of things that are longer than 1 km.
2. With help from a friend, measure the length of your shadow in centimeters at 9:00 A.M., noon, and 2:00 P.M. on the same day.

Chapter 6

Energy and Machines

All these farmers are doing work. Some of the farmers are using machines that pick up wheat in the field. These machines use energy supplied by their engines. The farmer in the smaller picture is also using a machine. It is called a pitchfork. The pitchfork picks up hay in the field. The pitchfork uses energy supplied by the farmer.

These farmers are using different machines to do similar types of work. Both machines use energy to do the work. But, as you can see, the machines are very different. In this chapter you will learn about different machines and how they do work. You will also learn about the energy needed by these machines.

FORMS OF ENERGY

What are some different forms of energy?

What do the crane and the baseball player have in common? They are both doing work. You might not think of hitting a baseball as work. However, work is done whenever a force is used to move an object. The boy is moving the ball by hitting it, or by giving it a quick push. The crane is moving boxes by lifting them.

It takes energy to do work. Energy does not take up space or have mass. So energy is not matter. **Energy** is the ability to do work. Cranes get energy from gasoline. People get energy from the food they eat. Gasoline and food contain chemical (kem'ə kəl) energy. Chemical energy is just one form of energy.

Suppose you could go to the fair shown here. What forms of energy could you find? Even before you got to the fair, you would notice two forms of energy. First you would be able to see the light bulbs on the rides. These light bulbs would be giving off light energy. As you got closer, you would hear another form of energy called sound energy.

The light bulbs at the fair would be lit by electrical (i lek'trə kəl) energy. The moving parts on the rides and games would have another form of energy. This form is called mechanical (mə kan'ə kəl) energy. Anything that moves has mechanical energy. If you got hungry at the fair, you might eat a hot dog or some popcorn. This food would have been cooked using heat energy. The light bulbs at the fair would also give off heat energy.

Did you know that energy can change from one form to another? Electrical energy can be changed to light energy and heat energy by light bulbs. Electrical energy can also be changed into sound energy by a radio.

You learned that chemical energy in gasoline can be used to make a crane move. To do this, chemical energy is burned to release heat energy. The heat energy is then changed to mechanical energy. Chemical energy stored in wood is changed to heat energy and light energy when the wood is burned. Chemical energy is also stored in fireworks. What forms of energy is the chemical energy changed into when the fireworks explode?

Light bulbs

Fire

Fireworks

TWO KINDS OF ENERGY

What are potential and kinetic energy?

How is work being done in this picture? The wrecking ball is doing work by moving the wall of the building. The ball must have a lot of energy to do this much work. The ball has a kind of energy called kinetic (ki-net′ik) energy. **Kinetic energy** is the energy of motion.

What if the wall could not be moved by this ball? How could the ball be changed and still knock down the wall? Swinging the ball faster would make the wall move. Or a heavier ball could do the job. Either way the ball would have more kinetic energy. The kinetic energy of an object depends on its mass and speed. If you increased the mass or the speed of the ball, you would increase its kinetic energy. If the ball had more energy, it could do more work.

As you have learned, anything that moves has mechanical energy. So mechanical energy is a type of kinetic energy. Some other forms of energy are also types of kinetic energy. Light energy, heat energy, and sound energy all move from one place to another. So they are all types of kinetic energy.

Just before this picture was taken, the man was not moving. So he did not have kinetic energy. But as the man swings on the rope, he moves. He has kinetic energy.

While the man holds the rope at the top of the hill, he has potential (pə ten'shəl) energy. **Potential energy** is stored energy. As he starts to move, this stored energy will begin to change to kinetic energy. When he reaches the bottom of his swing, he will have a lot of kinetic energy. He will have little potential energy. Most of his potential energy will have changed into kinetic energy.

Some of the forms of energy you have read about are also types of potential energy. For example, a battery has chemical potential energy. The chemical energy is stored until the battery is connected in a circuit. Then it is changed to electrical energy. This electrical energy might be used to light a light bulb. A piece of wood has chemical potential energy. The chemical energy is stored until the wood is burned. What happens to it then?

How is the height of a swinging mass related to its energy?

Materials   C-clamp / 50-g mass / string / block of wood / meterstick

Procedure

A. Tie one end of the string to a 50-g mass.

B. Clamp a C-clamp to the edge of a table. Tie the loose end of the string to the C-clamp.

C. Adjust the string so that the mass almost touches the floor. Make a small pencil mark on the floor under the mass. Set a block of wood on the mark.

D. Pull back the mass until it is exactly 10 cm above the floor.
   1. Predict how far the block will move when it is struck by the mass.

E. Let the mass swing down and hit the block. Measure how far it moves from the mark on the floor.
   2. How far did the block move?
   3. How does this compare with your prediction?

F. Repeat step **E**, pulling the mass 20 cm, 30 cm, 40 cm, and 50 cm above the floor.
   4. Predict how far the block will move each time.
   5. How far did the block move each time?

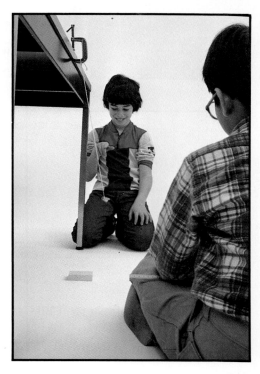

Conclusion
How is the height of the mass related to the amount of work done?

Using science ideas
Make a bar graph of your results.

-SIMPLE MACHINES AND ENERGY-
How is energy used by different simple machines?

Have you ever tried to lift a car? Probably not. A car is very heavy. Lifting even one end of a car would be a lot of work. Yet this man is lifting a car. He is able to do this by using a jack. A jack consists of a simple machine called a lever. A **simple machine** is a machine made of very few parts.

A **lever** is a machine made of a bar or rod that turns on a point. The point on which a lever turns is called the fulcrum. A force, or effort, is used on one end of the lever. This force moves an object that is attached to the other end. This object is called the load. The closer the fulcrum is to the load, the easier the load is to lift.

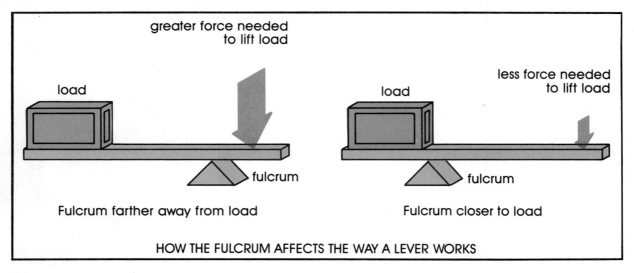

greater force needed to lift load

less force needed to lift load

load

load

fulcrum

fulcrum

Fulcrum farther away from load

Fulcrum closer to load

HOW THE FULCRUM AFFECTS THE WAY A LEVER WORKS

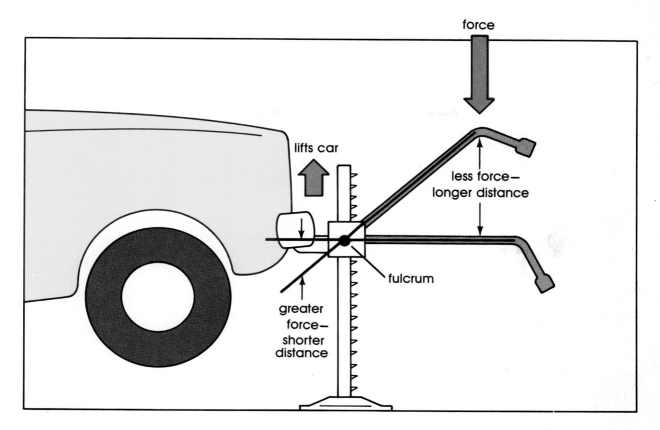

force

lifts car

less force—
longer distance

greater
force—
shorter
distance

fulcrum

Even though using a lever makes work easier, it does not save energy. Look at the drawing of the car jack. It takes less force to push down on the jack handle than it would take to lift the car by hand. But you have to push the handle a long distance to lift the car a short distance. If you move the handle 40 cm, the car may be lifted only 2 cm. So why use a car jack? The answer is to decrease the force needed to lift the heavy car. The only way you can lift the car is to decrease the force. The jack is a simple machine that decreases the force needed to lift the car. That is the advantage of a simple machine.

How does changing the fulcrum affect a lever?

Materials   meterstick / large pencil / metric masses

Procedure

A. Make a lever by laying a meterstick across a large pencil. The pencil will act as the fulcrum in your lever. Place the pencil under the 50-cm mark on the meterstick.

B. Place a 10-g mass between the end of the meterstick and the 1-cm mark. Add enough masses between the 99-cm and 100-cm marks to balance the lever.
   1. How much mass did it take to balance the 10-g mass?

C. Repeat step **B** with the fulcrum at the 60-cm mark, the 70-cm mark, and the 80-cm mark.
   2. How much mass did it take to balance the 10-g mass each time?

Conclusion

1. What happens to the amount of mass needed to balance the lever as the fulcrum is moved farther away from the 10-g mass?
2. If you were using a lever to lift a heavy load, how would you position the fulcrum to make the job easier?

Using science ideas

Use the information from the activity to make a pictograph.

Another type of simple machine is called a wheel and axle. A **wheel and axle** consists of a wheel connected to an axle. When either the wheel or the axle moves, the other moves, too.

A doorknob is a wheel and axle. Have you ever tried to open a door by just turning the axle of a doorknob? It takes a large force to do this. By attaching a larger handle to the axle, less force is needed. But, as with levers, this force is used over a long distance. So a wheel and axle does not save energy.

axle

wheel

This ramp is a third kind of simple machine called an inclined plane. An **inclined plane** is a machine made of a slanted surface. Pushing the box up the inclined plane takes a small force. Lifting the box straight up takes a larger force. But the distance the box is pushed across the inclined plane is long. The distance the box would be lifted is shorter. The smaller force needed to push the box is used over a long distance. The larger force needed to lift the box is used over a shorter distance. Inclined planes make work easier without saving energy.

A pulley is still another type of simple machine. A **pulley** is made of a wheel that has a groove in it. A rope, chain, or belt fits into the groove. Pulleys can be used in two ways. The pulley used on a flagpole is a fixed pulley. A fixed pulley can change the direction of your force. You pull down on one end of the rope. The load is pulled up by the other end. It takes the same force to lift a load with a fixed pulley as it does without a fixed pulley.

direction in which load moves

direction in which force moves

Fixed pulley

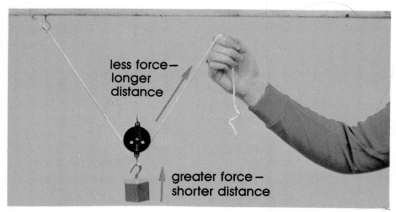

less force— longer distance

greater force— shorter distance

Movable pulley

The pulley shown above is a movable pulley. A movable pulley does not change the direction of your force. Like a lever, a movable pulley lets you use less force to lift a load. But you must pull the rope a longer distance than the load moves. The smaller force needed to lift a load with a movable pulley is used over a longer distance. So a movable pulley does not save energy.

Not all the energy you put into a machine is used to move a load. A small part of the energy is used to overcome a force called friction (frik′shən). **Friction** is a force that slows down or stops motion. There is friction when two parts of a machine rub against each other. In the inclined plane there is friction between the box and the surface of the ramp. In the pulley there is some friction between the rope and the wheel of the pulley.

One way to reduce friction is by covering surfaces that rub together with grease or oil. Another way is by using wheels. A box with wheels can be pushed up a ramp much easier than can a box without wheels.

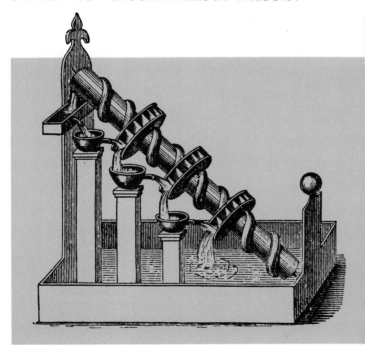

Do you know?

For hundreds of years people have tried to build a perpetual (pər pech′ ú əl) motion machine. A perpetual motion machine is a machine that would never stop working once it was set in motion. Such a machine would not need an outside source of energy. It could produce its own energy forever.

Many plans for perpetual motion machines have been drawn. But friction has stopped every machine from working forever.

— COMPOUND MACHINES AND — ENERGY
What is a compound machine?

How many simple machines can you name in this can opener? The two long handles are levers. The key that you turn to open a can is a wheel and axle. The cutting blade is a type of inclined plane. A can opener is made of many simple machines. Any machine that is made up of two or more simple machines is called a **compound machine**.

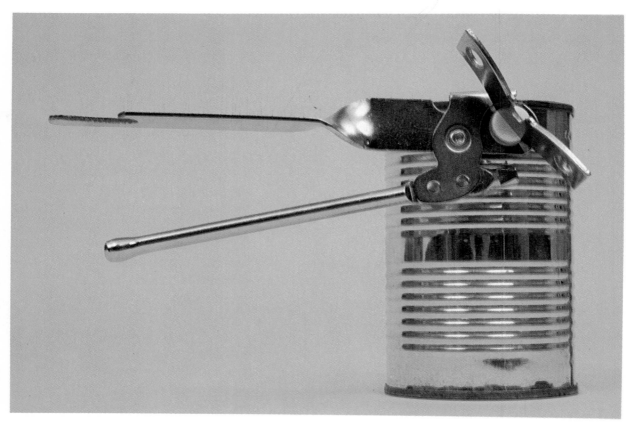

There are many different kinds of compound machines. Some, such as a wheelbarrow, are made up of only a few simple machines. Other compound machines, such as a car, are made of hundreds of wheels, levers, and pulleys. Some compound machines, such as a wheelbarrow, use mechanical energy. Others, such as a car, use chemical energy.

A bicycle is a compound machine. Study the bicycle shown here. How many simple machines can you name?

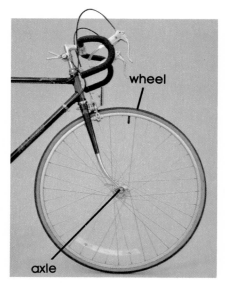

wheel

axle

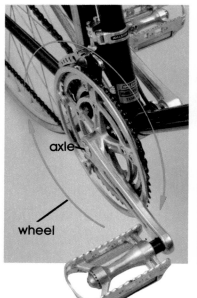

axle

wheel

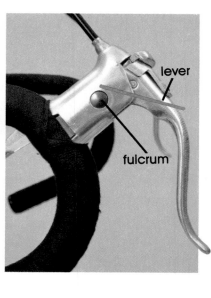

lever

fulcrum

wheel

axle

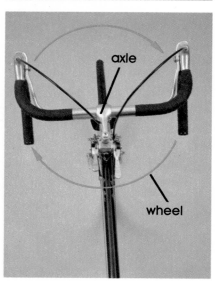

axle

wheel

A bicycle is made of many simple machines. There are several wheel-and-axle machines on this bicycle. The wheels of the bicycle are connected to axles. So they form a wheel-and-axle machine. The pedals are two other wheel-and-axle machines. First the pedals turn a gear. This gear is connected to a gear on the rear wheel of the bicycle by a chain. The gears and the chain that connects them form a third wheel-and-axle machine. The handlebars make up a fourth wheel and axle. This bicycle also has brake handles, which are levers. These levers help to make it easier to stop the bicycle. Where does the energy used by each of these simple machines come from?

Finding out

What simple machines can you identify in different compound machines? See how many simple machines you can find in different compound machines. You may use some of the compound machines shown here, or others that you find in your home or classroom. For each simple machine you find, decide what job it does in the compound machine. How would the compound machine work if the simple machine were removed? How does the simple machine get the energy it uses?

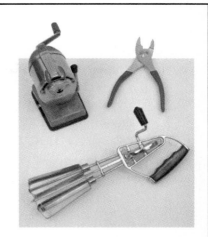

IDEAS TO REMEMBER

► Energy is the ability to do work. Chemical energy, light energy, sound energy, heat energy, electrical energy, and mechanical energy are different forms of energy.

► The energy of motion is called kinetic energy. Stored energy is called potential energy.

► A simple machine is a machine made of very few parts. A lever, an inclined plane, a wheel and axle, and a pulley are simple machines.

► A simple machine makes it easier to do work, but it does not save energy.

► A compound machine is a machine made of two or more simple machines.

Reviewing the Chapter

SCIENCE WORDS

A. Use the science terms to identify the following.

compound machine	pulley	simple machine
inclined plane	lever	wheel and axle

1. I am any machine made of very few parts. What am I?
2. I am a machine made of a slanted surface. What am I?
3. I am any machine made up of two or more other machines. What am I?
4. I am a machine made of a bar or rod that turns on a point. What am I?
5. I am a machine made of a wheel connected to an axle. What am I?
6. I am a machine made of a wheel that has a groove in it. A rope, chain, or belt fits into this groove. What am I?

B. Copy the sentences below. Use science terms from the chapter to complete the sentences.

1. The energy of motion is called ____.
2. Stored energy is called ____.
3. A force that works to keep one object from sliding across another is called ____.
4. The ability to do work is called ____.
5. Light bulbs are lit by energy called ____.

UNDERSTANDING IDEAS

A. Explain the difference between kinetic energy and potential energy. Use examples in your answer.

B. Identify at least one form of energy in each of these pictures. Explain how one of the forms of energy comes from another form of energy.

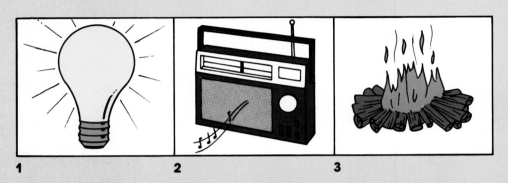

1   2   3

C. Explain why a simple machine makes work easier to do but does not save energy. Use a lever in your explanation.

USING IDEAS

1. Make a list of different forms of energy in your home. Identify which forms of energy come from other forms of energy.
2. Find out how changing the angle of an inclined plane changes the force needed to move an object up it.
3. As you learned in this chapter, some of the energy put into a machine is used to overcome friction. Yet friction is helpful in many ways. Describe what the world would be like if there were no friction.

Chapter 7

Heat Energy

When you first look at this picture, you might not think of heat. All you see is a cold winter scene. But look closely at the picture. What sign that heat is present can you see?

Some people are wearing heavy clothing. They are trying not to lose their body heat. One person has removed his jacket, hat, and gloves. He is losing body heat. What source of energy is keeping him warm?

In this chapter you will learn about heat energy. You will also learn how heat moves from one place to another.

HEAT
What is heat?

In what ways have you experienced heat? Maybe you can remember hot summer days when you played in the shade all day. You might remember trying to cool some hot soup before you ate it. Or maybe you have felt the warmth of a campfire.

As you can see, heat can be experienced in many ways. But what is heat? **Heat** is a form of energy. As more heat energy is added to matter, it becomes hotter. For example, if you add more heat energy to a pot of soup, it will become hotter.

particles moving fast

particles moving slowly

hot soup

cold milk

All matter is made up of tiny moving particles. The more heat energy that matter has, the faster the particles move. For example, hot soup has a lot of heat energy. The particles that make up hot soup move fast. Cold milk has little heat energy. The particles in cold milk move slowly.

Heat energy is measured by the effect it has on matter. Heat affects matter by raising the temperature of matter. Think of two cups filled with the same amount of water at 0°C. One cup is heated to 10°C. The other cup is heated to 20°C. Which cup has received the most heat energy?

Heat energy is measured in a unit called a calorie (kal′ər ē). Adding calories of heat to matter will raise the temperature of matter. The water heated to 20°C needs two times more calories than water heated to 10°C.

When you think of heat, you often think about temperature (tem'pər ə chər). Heat and temperature seem to go together. As you have learned, heat causes the particles in matter to move faster. **Temperature** is a measure of the speed of the particles. The faster the particles in matter move, the higher the temperature of the matter. Temperature, then, is a measure of how hot or cold matter is.

Do you know?

The next time you have your temperature taken, one of these new types of thermometers may be used. Thermometers **A** and **D** are made from plastic. Thermometer **A** is held against your forehead. Thermometer **D** is held under your tongue. Your temperature shows up as a change in color on each of these thermometers. Thermometers **B** and **C** use a small probe held under the tongue. Your temperature is read on a small screen with thermometer **C** and on a dial with thermometer **B**.

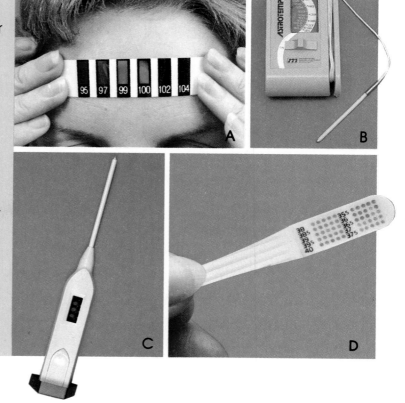

Pleasant summer day—27°C

Ice—0°C

Temperature can be measured in units called **degrees Celsius** (di grēz′ sel′sē əs). The symbol for degrees Celsius is °C. Boiling water has a temperature of 100°C. Ice has a temperature of 0°C. On a pleasant summer day, the temperature might be 27°C.

Boiling water—100°C

Finding out

What is the difference in temperature of different forms of water? Fill a bowl halfway with cold tap water. Put the bulb end of a Celsius thermometer into the water. Wait until the level of the liquid in the thermometer stops changing. Then read the thermometer. Repeat these steps with hot tap water and then with crushed ice. What is the difference in temperature between these three bowls of water?

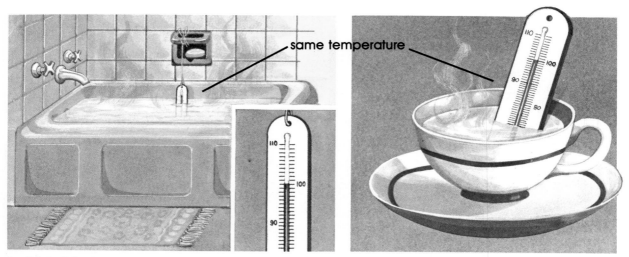

bathtub full of boiling water:
more particles—more heat

teacup full of boiling water:
fewer particles—less heat

To see how temperature is different from heat, think of this example. Suppose you have a bathtub and a teacup, each full of boiling water. The water in the bathtub and the teacup would be at the same temperature. So the particles of water in each would be moving at the same speed. But there are far more particles of water in the bathtub than in the teacup. The water in the bathtub could also warm the cool air in a small room. The water in the teacup would have little effect on the air in the room. So the water in the bathtub contains more heat than does the water in the teacup.

As you can see, two objects can have the same temperature. But if one of the objects is larger than the other, it will have more heat.

HOW HEAT MOVES THROUGH SOLID MATTER

How does heat move through a solid?

Have you ever touched a metal spoon that has been in hot soup for a time? The handle of the spoon was probably hot. Heat moved from the soup to the spoon. How did this happen?

Suppose you could see the particles of matter in the spoon and in the soup. A spoon is a solid. Particles of matter in a solid vibrate (vī'brāt), or move back and forth. But the particles do not move around. Soup is a liquid. Particles of matter in a liquid are free both to vibrate and to move around. In the following drawing you can see how the particles in the spoon and the soup move.

particles
in soup
moving fast

particles
in spoon
vibrating

The particles of matter in the hot soup have a lot of energy. They are moving quickly. The particles in the spoon have less energy. They are vibrating slowly. Some particles of matter in the soup hit some particles of matter in the spoon. The particles in the spoon that were hit begin to vibrate faster. These particles hit other particles in the spoon, causing the other particles to vibrate faster. This keeps happening all along the handle of the spoon. The heat energy is being passed from particle to particle along the handle. The way heat energy moves through a solid is called **conduction** (kən duk′shən).

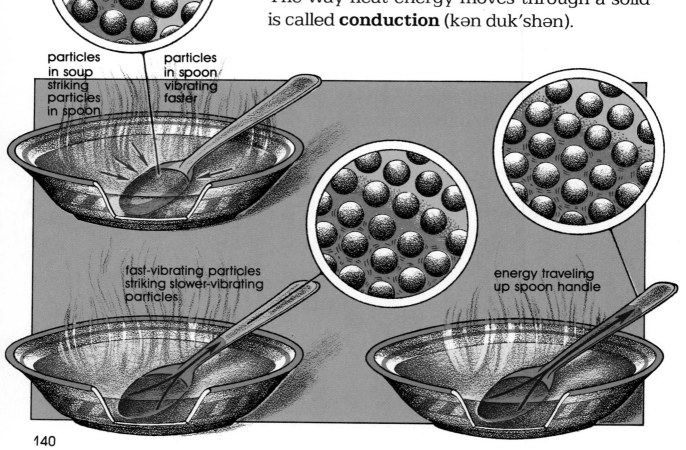

particles in soup striking particles in spoon

particles in spoon vibrating faster

fast-vibrating particles striking slower-vibrating particles

energy traveling up spoon handle

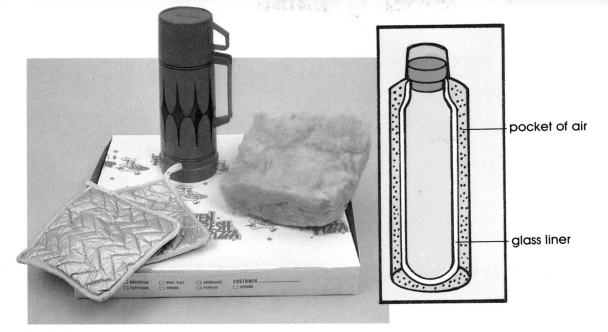

pocket of air

glass liner

Insulators

Heat energy does not move at the same speed through all kinds of matter. Heat energy cannot move easily through some materials. These materials are called good **insulators** (in'sə lā tərs). The particles that make up a good insulator are spaced far apart. The pizza box, pot holders, and home insulation shown above are made of good insulating materials. So is the thermos. It uses a layer of air to keep hot liquids hot and cold liquids cold. Particles of air are spaced far apart.

Heat energy can easily move through other materials. These materials are called good **conductors** (kən duk'tərs). The particles that make up a good conductor are close together. The pans and iron shown here are made of good conducting materials.

Conductors

141

What fabrics make good insulators?

	WATER TEMPERATURE	
	At beginning	After 30 min.
Jar wrapped with cotton cloth		
Jar wrapped with wool cloth		
Jar wrapped with polyester cloth		
Unwrapped jar		

Materials 4 identical jars with lids / hot tap water / 4 thermometers / tape / pieces of cotton, wool, and polyester cloth

Procedure

A. Make a chart like the one shown.

B. Half fill four identical jars with hot tap water.

C. Place a thermometer in each jar. Measure the temperature of the water in each jar. Make sure the temperatures are about the same. Write the temperatures in the chart.

D. Screw the lid tightly on each jar.

E. Cover three of the jars with pieces of cloth. Wrap a piece of cotton cloth around one jar. Wrap a piece of wool cloth around the second jar and a piece of polyester cloth around the third jar. Fasten each piece of cloth with a piece of tape.

F. Unwrap the jars after 30 minutes. Read the thermometers. Write the temperatures in the chart.

Conclusion

1. The cloth covering the jar whose water temperature fell the least was the best insulator. Which cloth was the best insulator?

2. The cloth covering the jar whose water temperature fell the most was the poorest insulator. Which cloth was the poorest insulator?

Using science ideas

Make a graph to show the difference in temperature of each jar.

—HOW HEAT MOVES THROUGH— LIQUIDS AND GASES
What is convection?

Heat energy can easily move through conductors. But most liquids and gases are not good conductors. So how does heat move through liquids and gases?

The way heat energy moves through liquids and gases is called **convection** (kən-vek'shən). Like conduction, convection is caused by the movement of particles in matter. But unlike conduction, in convection the particles move from one place to another.

To help you understand convection, think of a room in a house. The room contains a radiator. How is the entire room heated by one radiator?

Look at the picture below. As you can see, at first only the air near the radiator is heated. As this air becomes warmer, the particles that make up the air begin to move faster. The particles also move farther apart. So the warm air takes up more space. The air is less dense than it was before it was heated.

Because the warm air is less dense, it rises toward the ceiling. Cooler, heavier air moves down to replace the warmer air. The cool air is then heated by the radiator. It, too, begins to rise. A river of moving air is set up. This river carries heat throughout the room. In this way the room is heated by convection.

cooler air moving down

warm air beginning to rise

air becoming warm

HEAT FROM SUNLIGHT

How does the sun warm matter on earth?

Have you ever been warmed by the sun on a cold day? As long as you stayed in the sunlight, you were warm. If the sun went behind a cloud, you were chilly. Why did this happen?

As you can see in the drawing, the sun gives off other forms of energy besides light. These forms of energy cannot be seen. But like light, the other forms of energy travel in waves. One of the other forms of energy changes to heat when it strikes matter. The movement of heat energy in waves is called **radiation** (rā dē ā'shən).

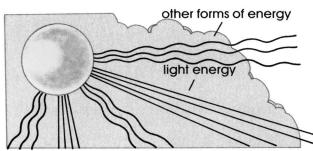

light energy and other forms of energy leaving sun

waves of energy striking matter changing to heat

Your body is made of matter. When you stand in sunlight, waves of energy from the sun strike you. Some of the energy changes to heat. You are warmed by the heat. This is why you can be warmed by the sun on a cold day.

Can glass trap heat from the sun?

Materials   2 thermometers / glass jar with lid

Procedure

A. Make a chart like the one shown.

B. Place a thermometer in a glass jar. Screw the lid on tightly.

C. Place the jar in direct sunlight on a table or windowsill. Place a second thermometer next to the jar. Read both thermometers. Write the temperatures under the heading *0 minutes.*

D. Read the thermometers every 5 minutes for 20 minutes. Write the temperatures in the chart.

Conclusion

1. What happened to the temperature inside the glass jar during the 20-minute period?

2. What happened to the temperature outside the jar during the same time?

3. Which temperature was higher after 20 minutes?

4. Did the glass jar trap heat from the sun?

Using science ideas

Some people are beginning to use heat from the sun to heat their homes. Find out about solar collectors. How are they like the jar you used in this activity? How are they different?

Time	Temperature inside jar	Temperature outside jar
0 min.		
5 min.		
10 min.		
15 min.		
20 min.		

Have you ever seen a greenhouse? Much of the heat in a greenhouse comes from the sun. Waves of energy from the sun travel through the glass roof of the greenhouse. When the waves strike matter inside the greenhouse, they change to heat. Heat cannot escape through the glass, so the heat gets trapped inside. This warms the greenhouse. A greenhouse can be warmed even on the coldest day of winter. Have you ever entered a closed-up car that was sitting in the sun? Why was the inside of the car very hot?

Greenhouse

IDEAS TO REMEMBER

▶ Heat is a form of energy measured in calories.
▶ Temperature is a measure of how hot or cold matter is.
▶ The way heat energy moves through a solid is called conduction.
▶ The way heat energy moves through a liquid or gas is called convection.
▶ The movement of heat energy in waves is called radiation.

Reviewing the Chapter

SCIENCE WORDS

A. Use all the terms below to complete the sentences.

convection   conduction   insulator
conductor   radiation

      Heat energy moves in different ways through different kinds of matter. The way heat energy moves through a solid is called __**1**__. Heat energy does not move at the same speed through all kinds of solids. Heat energy can easily move through a type of solid called a/an __**2**__. Heat energy cannot easily move through another type of solid called a/an __**3**__. The way heat energy moves through liquids and gases is called __**4**__. Heat energy also comes from waves of energy from the sun. This movement of heat energy in waves is called __**5**__.

B. Write the letter of the term that best matches the definition. Not all the terms will be used.

1. A unit of energy	**a.** heat
2. A measure of how hot or cold matter is	**b.** conductor
3. A form of energy	**c.** calorie
4. A unit used to measure temperature	**d.** degree Celsius
	e. temperature

UNDERSTANDING IDEAS

A. Look at the drawing. Draw what the particles that make up liquid A and liquid B would look like.

A

B

B. Which cup of soup needed more calories to get hot? Explain your answer.

A

B

C. Explain the difference between an insulator and a conductor. Use examples in your explanation.

D. Copy the following groups of terms. Cross out the term that does not belong in each group. Then describe what the remaining terms have in common.

1. thermometer, degrees Celsius, heat, temperature
2. solid, insulator, conduction, convection
3. convection, liquid, conduction, gas
4. insulator, radiation, waves, sun

USING IDEAS

1. Make a list of the different insulators and conductors found in your home.

Chapter 8

Electricity and Magnetism

On a hot summer evening in 1965, the electricity went off in the city of New York. All the lights went out. Crowded subways and elevators stopped where they were. Refrigerators and air conditioners shut off. The entire city was without electricity for several hours.

People in New York found that it was difficult to live without electricity, even for a short time. Imagine what it would be like if there were no electricity in your town. How would your life be different?

In this chapter you will learn about different types of electricity. You will also learn how electricity is related to magnetism.

What is static electricity?

There are two types of electricity. One type is called current electricity. You use this type of electricity to light your home and classroom. The second type is called static electricity. **Static electricity** is made by friction, or rubbing. Static electricity makes your hair rise when you pull a sweater over your head. It also causes lightning. But what causes static electricity?

All matter is made up of tiny particles that have electric charges. Some of these particles have a positive charge. Other particles have a negative charge. Rubbing two objects together may cause some of the negative charges to rub off one object. The charges move to the second object. This gives the second object a greater negative charge than the first object.

1 negative and positive charges on both sweater and hair

2 negative charges from sweater moving to hair

What happens when you pull off a sweater over your head? Look at the drawings. As you take off the sweater, you rub off some of the negative charges from the sweater. These negative charges move to your hair. Now your hair has more negative charges than your sweater does. Your sweater has more positive charges than negative charges. Negative and positive charges attract each other, or are drawn together. So the positive charges from the sweater attract the negative charges on your hair. This makes your hair rise.

Can you name other ways you have experienced static electricity? Static electricity causes clothes to stick to each other in a clothes dryer. You can also experience static electricity while you comb your hair. Try combing your hair, and then hold the comb close to your hair. What happens? Why does this happen?

3 positive charges on sweater attracting negative charges on hair

How do charged objects act toward each other?

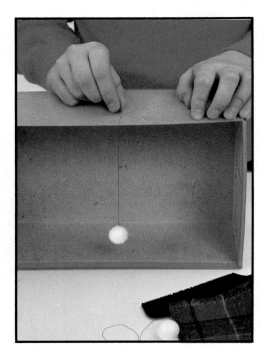

Materials 2 plastic-foam balls / tape / thread / shoebox / comb / wool cloth

Procedure

A. Tape a plastic-foam ball to one end of a piece of thread. Tape the other end of the thread to a shoebox as shown.

B. Rub a comb with a wool cloth. This gives the comb a negative charge.
   1. Predict what will happen if you bring the comb near the ball.

C. Bring the comb near the ball.
   2. What happens?
   3. Is the charge on the ball the same as the charge on the comb? How do you know?

D. Tape another ball to a second piece of thread. Hang this ball next to the first ball. Make sure the balls are touching.

E. Rub the comb with the cloth again. Predict what will happen when you bring the comb near one of the balls. Now try it.
   4. What happens?
   5. What kind of charge must each of the balls have for this to happen? How do you know?

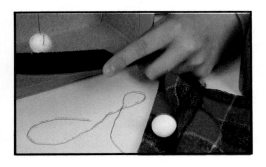

Conclusion

1. What happens when an object that has one type of charge is brought near an object that has the opposite charge?

2. What happens when an object that has one type of charge is brought near an object that has the same type of charge?

CURRENT ELECTRICITY

How is current electricity produced?

Whenever you turn on a television, a radio, or a lamp, you are using current electricity. **Current electricity** is produced when negative charges flow along a path. How is this different from static electricity?

The path along which negative charges flow is called a **circuit** (sėr'kit). The picture shows four parts of an electric circuit. (1) There is a source of electricity. In this circuit the source of electricity is a battery. (2) There is a path along which charges can flow. In this circuit a wire forms the path. (3) There is a switch that opens and closes the circuit. (4) There is some object that uses the electricity. In this circuit the object is a light bulb.

AN ELECTRIC CIRCUIT

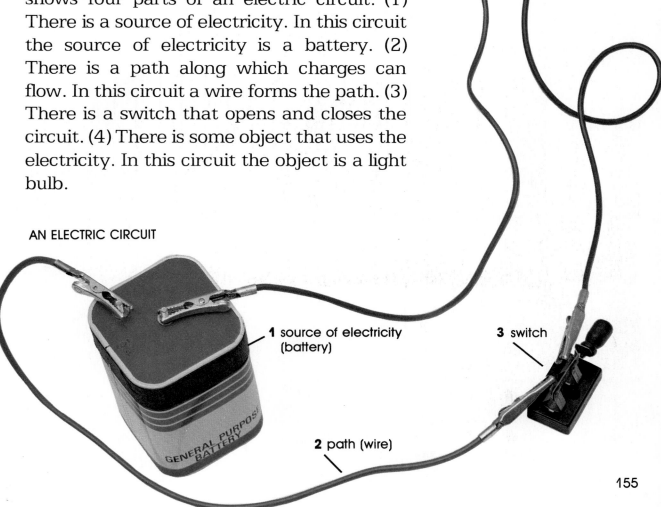

4 user of electricity (light bulb)

1 source of electricity (battery)

3 switch

2 path (wire)

In this electric circuit the charges flow from the battery, through the wire, to the switch. Then they flow through the light bulb and back to the battery. When the switch is closed, or turned on, the path is complete. The charges can flow. A circuit whose path is complete is called a **complete circuit.** When the switch is open, or turned off, the path is broken. The flow of charges stops. The path is incomplete. A circuit whose path is incomplete is called an **incomplete circuit.**

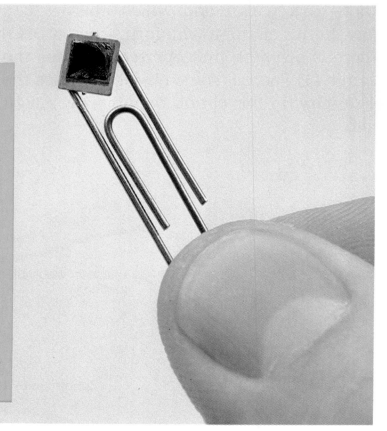

Do you know?

Circuits can be used to store huge amounts of information. They can even be used to solve problems. You would think these circuits are very large. But you might be surprised to know they are smaller than a paper clip. These circuits are found on tiny chips called microchips. Electricity moving through these circuits can be used to do many special jobs. Microchips are found in computers and many other machines.

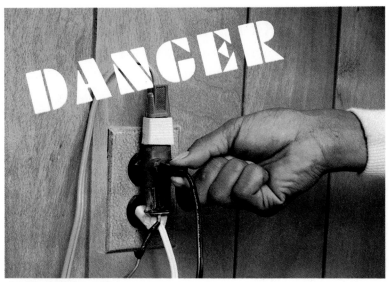

Overloaded outlet

Electricity is useful, but it can also be dangerous. Electric wires should be handled carefully. If the outer covering of an electric wire is cracked or peeled, you can get a shock. Because of this, electric wires should never be pulled, stretched, or moved more than necessary.

Heat is produced as electricity flows through wires. If too many wires are plugged into one outlet, too much heat is produced. This can cause a fire.

Fires can also be caused by a short circuit. A short circuit can happen when the outer covering of the wires is worn and the wires touch each other. You can prevent short circuits by not using old or worn electric wires. Short circuits can also be prevented by handling all electric wires carefully.

MAKING ELECTRICITY
What are some ways electricity can be made?

This flashlight needs electricity to work. The electricity used by a flashlight comes from a battery. A **battery** is an object that changes chemical energy into electricity.

There are two types of batteries. A dry cell battery is the type of battery used in a flashlight. A **dry cell battery** is a battery that is made up of a zinc case with a carbon rod in the center. The space in between is filled with a chemical paste. A chemical reaction takes place inside the battery. The reaction produces electric charges. Turning on a switch connects the zinc and the carbon. They form a circuit through which charges can move. The moving charges light the bulb.

light bulb

carbon rod

zinc case

paste

dry cell battery

wire

PARTS OF A FLASHLIGHT

The electricity from a car battery also comes from chemical action. A car battery is a wet cell battery. A **wet cell battery** is a battery that is made of layers of lead instead of zinc and carbon. The case has water and acid in it instead of paste. The lead and acid cause a chemical action that produces electricity.

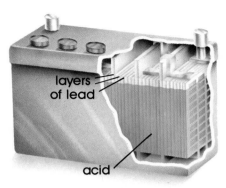

Hydroelectric power plant

Electricity can also be produced by a generator (jen'ə rā tər). A **generator** is a machine that uses a magnet to make electricity. Power plants use large generators to make electricity for whole towns. Generators have moving parts. They need a source of energy to move the parts. The generator in the power plant shown above uses moving water. This kind of power plant is called a hydroelectric (hī drō i lek'trik) power plant.

159

MAGNETISM
What is a magnet?

Have you ever used a magnet? If you have, you know that a **magnet** is an object that attracts metals, such as iron and steel. You may also know that a magnetic force can be found in the space around a magnet. This space is called the **magnetic field.** A magnetic field can be seen when iron filings are sprinkled near a magnet. The iron filings form a pattern of lines. These lines are called lines of force. Lines of force show where the magnetic field is and what it looks like.

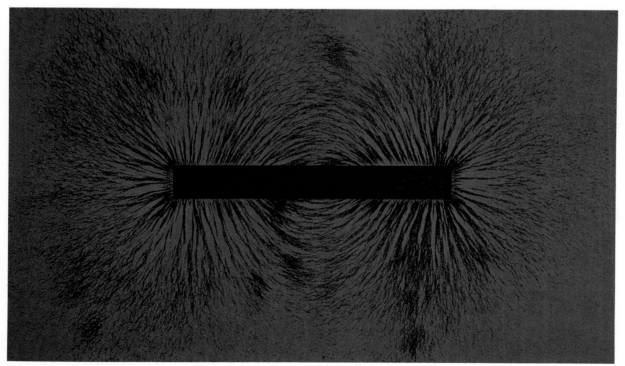

Magnetic field of one magnet

Magnetic field of two poles that are alike

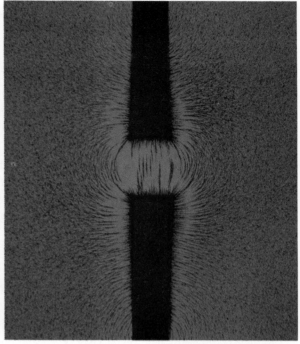

Magnetic field of two poles that are not alike

The ends of a magnet are called the **poles.** A magnetic field is strongest at the poles. A magnet has two poles—a north pole and a south pole. The poles are equal in strength. Do you know how the poles are different from each other?

The north pole of one magnet attracts the south pole of another magnet. The south pole of one magnet attracts the north pole of another magnet. But the north pole of one magnet repels, or pushes away, the north pole of another magnet. In the same way, the south pole of one magnet repels the south pole of a second magnet.

Finding out

How can you make a compass? A compass is used to show direction. It has a needle that is a magnet. One end of the needle always points to the north. By looking at a compass, you can tell which direction is north.

You can make a compass by using a small bar magnet. Identify the north pole of the magnet. Use a piece of tape to mark the north pole on the magnet. Center the magnet on a piece of plastic foam. Next fill a shallow aluminum tray with water. Add 20 drops of liquid soap to the water. Carefully place the magnet and plastic foam on the water. In which direction does the north pole of the magnet point? Slowly turn the tray of water so that it points in another direction. What happens to the magnet? How could you use your compass to find which direction is south?

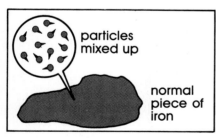

particles mixed up

normal piece of iron

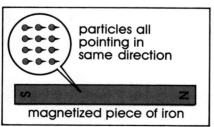

particles all pointing in same direction

magnetized piece of iron

What makes a magnet magnetic? Most magnets are made of iron. The particles that make up iron are like tiny magnets. Look at the first drawing. It is a normal piece of iron. As you can see, the particles are all mixed up. Each one points in a different direction. Now look at the second picture. It is a magnetized piece of iron. All the particles point in the same direction. Can you think of any way you could make a magnet out of a piece of iron?

What does a magnetic field look like?

Materials 2 bar magnets / piece of thin cardboard / iron filings

Procedure

A. Place a bar magnet on a table. Cover the magnet with a piece of thin cardboard.

B. Sprinkle iron filings on the cardboard. Tap the side of the cardboard gently.
  1. Make a drawing of the pattern formed by the iron filings.

C. Carefully place another magnet under the cardboard. The north poles of the two magnets should be next to each other. Tap the side of the cardboard gently.
  2. Make a drawing of the new pattern.

D. Now arrange the magnets so that the north pole of one magnet is next to the south pole of the other magnet. Tap the cardboard again.
  3. Make a drawing of the new pattern.

Conclusion

1. Iron filings line up along the magnetic field of a magnet. Describe the magnetic field of a magnet.

2. Describe the magnetic field of two magnets whose same poles are next to each other.

3. Describe the magnetic field of two magnets whose opposite poles are next to each other.

Using science ideas

Repeat steps **A** and **B** using different-shaped magnets.

— ELECTRICITY AND MAGNETISM —
What is an electromagnet?

Did you know that electricity and magnetism are related? First of all, magnetism can be used to produce electricity. This can be done by moving a magnet through a coil of wire. Electricity is produced as long as the magnet moves through the coil. A generator produces electricity in this way.

Electric current can be used to make a magnet. This can be done by wrapping wire around an iron nail. When electricity flows through the wire, a magnetic field is formed around the nail. The nail becomes a magnet. This type of magnet is called an electromagnet (i lek trō mag'nit). Electromagnets are often used in scrapyards to lift metal and move it. Many electromagnets are strong enough to lift heavy objects, such as cars. Electromagnets are also used in telephones.

Electromagnet in scrapyard

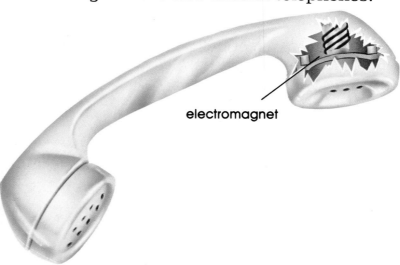

electromagnet

Finding out

How can you make an electromagnet? You can make an electromagnet by wrapping 90 cm of wire around a large nail. Be sure to make at least 20 turns around the nail. Then attach the free ends of the wire to the posts of a dry cell. Use your electromagnet to pick up paper clips. How many paper clips can you pick up? How could you make your electromagnet stronger without using a different source of electricity?

IDEAS TO REMEMBER

▶ Static electricity is electricity made by friction, or rubbing.

▶ Current electricity is produced when negative charges flow along a path called a circuit.

▶ Electricity can be produced using a battery or a generator.

▶ A magnet is an object that attracts metals, such as iron and steel.

▶ Magnetic poles that are alike repel, while magnetic poles that are not alike attract.

▶ Magnetism can be used to produce electricity. Electricity can be used to produce a magnet.

Reviewing the Chapter

SCIENCE WORDS

A. Write the letter of the term that best matches the definition. Not all the terms will be used.

1. The end of a magnet
2. Something produced when charges flow along a path
3. A battery made of lead, water, and acid
4. The space around a magnet in which a magnetic force can be found
5. An unbroken electrical path
6. Any object that changes chemical energy into electricity
7. A broken electrical path
8. A path along which negative charges flow

a. dry cell battery
b. magnetic field
c. incomplete circuit
d. pole
e. circuit
f. complete circuit
g. battery
h. current electricity
i. wet cell battery

B. Copy the sentences below. Use science terms from the chapter to complete each sentence.

1. A battery made of a zinc case with a carbon rod in the center is called a/an ____.
2. A/An ____ is a machine that uses a magnet to make electricity.
3. Electricity produced by friction is called ____.
4. A/An ____ is an object that attracts steel.

166

UNDERSTANDING IDEAS

A. Match each numbered item with its source of electricity.

1. car   **a.** power plant
2. flashlight   **b.** dry cell battery
3. town   **c.** wet cell battery

B. These two magnets are attracting each other. Identify poles 1, 2, and 3.

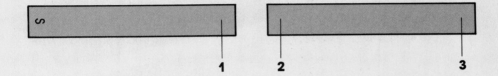

C. A girl rubbed a balloon with a piece of wool cloth. Then she held the balloon near her hair. She noticed that her hair was attracted to the balloon. Explain what happened.

USING IDEAS

1. Make a list of the different rooms in your home. Look for electrical outlets in each room. Write down what things are plugged into each outlet in each room.

2. Find out what objects around your home and school are attracted to a magnet. You can do this by touching different objects with a magnet. You might want to test a copper penny, an aluminum refrigerator, and an iron nail. Make lists of which objects were attracted to the magnet and which were not.

Science in Careers

Many people must do their jobs correctly before you can receive electricity in your home. Electricity is often used to supply heat and light and to run many machines found in your home.

After leaving the power plant, electricity travels along wires and enters your home. The electrical wires in your home were put in by *electricians*. Electricians must also make sure the wires are safe to use.

Power-plant mechanic

Electricity is usually produced at some type of power plant. The machines that produce electricity have been developed with the help of *engineers*. Engineers are also in charge of the power plant. *Operators* run the generators. *Mechanics* make the generators run smoothly.

Electrician

Some of the electricity in your home is used for lighting. Some of it may be used to provide heat. Heating equipment must be put in by *heating mechanics*. It must also be repaired by these mechanics.

People in Science

Lewis Latimer (1848–1928)

Lewis Latimer was born in Chelsea, Massachusetts. He was an engineer. His work with carbon led Thomas Edison to use the material in the first light bulb. Later, Latimer invented an easy way to attach the carbon to electric wires in the bulb. He also found a cheap method for making large numbers of these pieces of carbon. This lowered the cost of light bulbs.

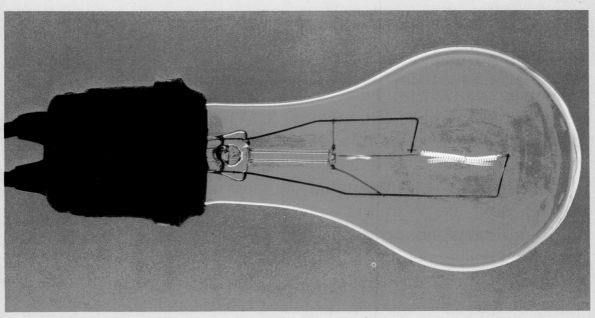

Light bulb

Developing Skills

WORD SKILLS

A prefix is one or more letters added to the beginning of a base word. A suffix is one or more letters added to the end of a base word. Prefixes and suffixes change the meanings of base words.

Prefix	Meaning	Example
bi-	two	bicycle
dis-	not	dislike
pre-	before	preview
un-	not	unnecessary

Use the tables to help you determine the meaning of each of the words listed. If you do not know the meaning of a base word, look it up in a dictionary.

1. bipolar
2. discharge
3. frictional
4. magnetize
5. preheat
6. unlighted

Suffix	Meaning	Example
-al	of, like	natural
-ize	cause to become	magnetize

READING A TABLE

The temperature at which a material melts is called its melting point. The temperature at which a material boils is called its boiling point. Use the table on the next page to answer these questions about melting points and boiling points.

1. Which material has the highest boiling point?
2. Which material has the highest melting point?
3. Which material has the lowest boiling point?
4. Which material has the lowest melting point?
5. Which material has a higher boiling point—iron or tin?
6. How much higher is the melting point of gold than the melting point of silver?

MELTING POINTS AND BOILING POINTS		
Material	Melting point	Boiling point
Aluminum	660°C	2,467°C
Calcium	842°C	1,487°C
Carbon	3,550°C	4,827°C
Copper	1,083°C	2,595°C
Gold	1,063°C	2,966°C
Iron	1,535°C	3,000°C
Lead	327°C	1,744°C
Nickel	1,453°C	2,732°C
Silver	961°C	2,212°C
Tin	232°C	2,270°C
Zinc	419°C	907°C

MAKING A TABLE

Measure the height of each member of your family. Make a table using these measurements. Who is the tallest member of your family? Who is the shortest member?

UNIT THREE

Learning About the Earth and the Planets

How would you describe what the earth is made of? You might say that the earth is made of rocks and soil. But oceans and lakes are also part of the earth. So is air, which makes up the earth's atmosphere.

To describe the earth, then, you would have to say that it consists of three main parts. It consists of rocks and soil making up the solid ground, liquid water in oceans and lakes, and gases in the atmosphere. Try to find each of these things in the pictures shown here.

In this unit you will find out more about the three main parts of the earth. You will also find out about the earth's neighbors— the planets.

Chapter 9

Rocks and Minerals

Imagine a beautiful, sunny day. You are flying in an airplane. As you look out the window, you see the land below. You notice that the earth is covered by rocks. You can see jagged rocks sticking out of the ocean. You see mountains formed by rocks. You can even see rocks partly covered with soil. There seem to be rocks everywhere.

Have you ever wondered how the rocks got there? Do you know that rocks can help us find out about plants and animals of long ago? Do you know some rocks are very valuable? In this unit you will take a closer look .at the earth and learn more about its rocks.

Big Sur, California

INSIDE THE EARTH

What are the three layers of the earth?

Like an apple, the earth has three layers. The crust of the earth is thin like the skin of an apple. The **crust** is an outer layer of rock that covers the whole earth. The crust is even found under the oceans. Here the crust is only 4 to 7 km thick. Mountains and valleys are part of the crust, too. On land the crust is about 35 km thick. We live on the earth's crust.

Under the crust is the mantle (man'təl). The **mantle** is the thickest layer of the earth. It is like the white part of the apple. No one has ever been able to drill through the crust to the mantle. Most scientists think the mantle is made of very hot rock.

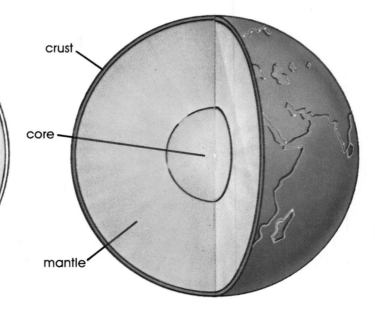

crust

core

mantle

Below the mantle is the core. The **core** is the inner layer of the earth. The core is like the core of the apple in the drawing. Many scientists believe that the core is made mostly of iron. They also believe it is so hot that much of the iron is liquid. Compare the crust, mantle, and core in the drawing on page 176. How are they different?

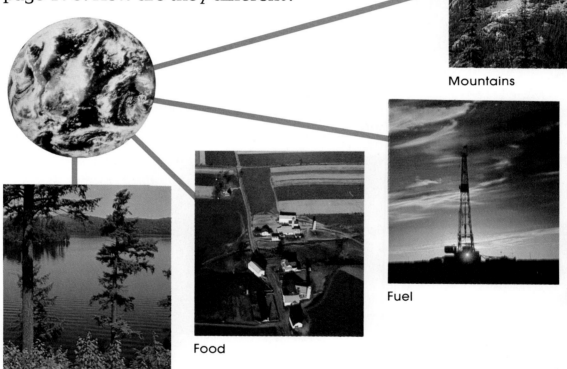

Mountains

Fuel

Food

Water

How is the earth important to us? The earth is important to us in many ways. We grow food in its soil. We drink the water it contains. It holds coal, oil, and gas, which we use as fuel. It also provides us with materials for making things.

MINERALS

What properties can be used to identify minerals?

Quartz crystals

Rocks are made up of one or more minerals (min′ər əlz). **Minerals** are pure solid materials found in the earth's crust. The particles that make up minerals join to form different-shaped crystals (kris′təlz). Different minerals can be identified by the shape of their crystals. A grain of salt is a crystal. If you look closely at salt, you will see little square blocks like those in the picture. These blocks are salt crystals.

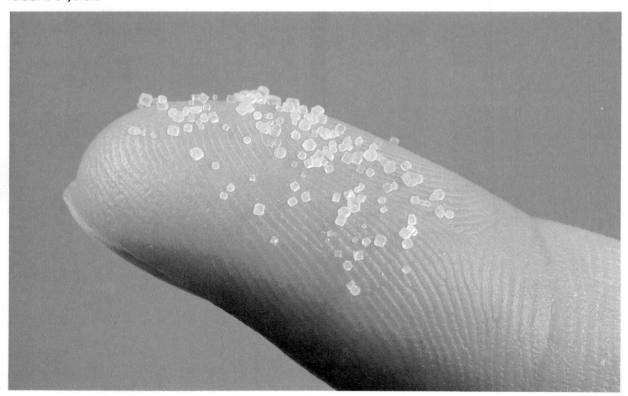

Salt crystals

There are hundreds of different minerals in the earth's crust. Each mineral has its own special properties. Scientists name, or identify, minerals by testing their properties. One property is magnetism. Magnetite (mag'nə tīt) is a magnetic mineral. Another property of a mineral is the shape of the crystals. You have already seen quartz and salt crystals. The color and the shine of the mineral are two other properties. Graphite (graf'īt) is black. Galena (gə lē'nə) is very shiny. Scientists often test for several properties before they are able to identify a mineral.

Graphite

Galena

The hardness of the mineral is another property used to identify it. Scientists test hardness by trying to scratch the mineral. Hardness is measured on a scale of 1 to 10.

The following table shows the hardness of some minerals. Have you ever seen any of these minerals?

MINERAL HARDNESS

Hardness	Mineral	
1 (Can be scratched with a fingernail)	TALC Talc is the softest mineral. It is used to make talcum powder.	
3 (Can be scratched with a copper penny)	CALCITE Calcite is used to make cement and fertilizer.	
7 (Can be scratched with a steel file)	QUARTZ Quartz is the most common mineral. It is used to make glass.	
10 (Can scratch glass)	DIAMOND A diamond is the hardest mineral. It cannot be scratched by any other mineral.	

MELTED ROCK

What are three ways rocks can form from melted rock?

It is very hot deep within the earth. It is so hot that the rock there is melted. Melted rock within the earth is called magma (mag′mə). Magma is found in the mantle of the earth. Sometimes it moves toward the surface through cracks in the crust.

Have you ever cooled a cup of hot water? If you cool water enough, it changes to solid ice. In a similar way, if magma cools enough, it changes to solid rock. Rocks formed from magma are called **igneous** (ig′nē əs) **rocks.**

When magma gets trapped in cracks below the earth's surface, it cools slowly. Rocks formed when magma cools slowly contain large crystals. Large crystals that make up a piece of granite (gran′it) are shown here.

Granite

Obsidian

Sometimes magma reaches the surface through a crack or opening in the earth. The magma that reaches the surface is called lava (lä′və). At the surface, lava cools and hardens quickly to form small crystals.

Some of the rocks formed by lava contain such tiny crystals that they look like glass. Obsidian (ob sid′ē ən) is a rock that looks like glass. Compare obsidian with the granite on page 181. How are they different?

Do you know?

Kilauea (kē lou ā ə) is a volcano in the Hawaiian Islands. It has been erupting, on and off, since January 1983. Unlike volcanoes on continents, island volcanoes are not so damaging. Kilauea sends rivers of hot, molten lava flowing down its sides. During major eruptions the rivers of lava flow into nearby villages. Trees, plants, and other things in the river's path are swallowed up by the hot lava. As the rivers of lava cool, smooth glassy rocks form.

The people of Hawaii are used to volcanoes. As volcanoes erupted below the ocean, layers of lava began to cool and harden. The islands are built from these layers of lava.

Volcano and a piece of pumice

Lava that shoots out of a volcano may have steam and gases in it. This lava can also cool very quickly. It can cool so quickly that the gases do not have time to escape. Pumice (pum'is) forms from this type of lava. The trapped gases leave the holes you can see in a piece of pumice. The holes make pumice a very light igneous rock. Pumice is so light that it floats in water.

How are crystals formed?

Materials   2 paper cups / string / 2 pencils / 2 pieces of paper, 3 cm × 6 cm / tape / ruler / hand lens

Procedure

A. Write your name on two pieces of paper. Write *Cooled slowly* on one. Write *Cooled quickly* on the other.

B. Tape each paper label to a different paper cup.

C. Use a ruler to measure the height of the paper cups. Tie a piece of string to each pencil. Cut the string 1 cm shorter than the height of the cups.

D. Rest the pencil on the cups as shown.

E. Ask your teacher to pour some hot sugar water into the cups.

F. Place the cup labeled *Cooled quickly* in a cold place. Place the cup labeled *Cooled slowly* in a warm place.
   1. Where would melted rock cool quickly on earth?
   2. Where would melted rock cool slowly?

G. After several days, remove the strings. Examine them with a hand lens. Compare the size of the crystals on each string.
   3. Describe the size of both sets of crystals.

Conclusion

1. What made the crystals form?
2. Why did one cup have larger crystals?
3. How does this activity show what happens in the earth to cooling magma?

ROCKS FROM SEDIMENT

How are sedimentary rocks formed?

A second type of rock is formed from sediment (sed'ə mənt). Sediment is material such as mud, sand, or gravel. Sediment is often carried by wind and water moving across land. Water from heavy rains or melting snows often carries sediment into rivers and streams. Rivers and streams carry the loose sediment to lakes and oceans, where it settles to the bottom. There the sediment builds up in layers. The heavy top layers press down on the bottom layers.

River depositing sediment in lake

After many years the sediment slowly hardens into a type of rock called sedimentary (sed ə men′tər ē) rock. A **sedimentary rock** is a rock formed from sediment. When you examine sedimentary rocks, you can often see the layers of sediment. Look at the layers in these sedimentary rocks.

Sedimentary rock layers

Finding out

How does sediment settle in water?   Get a large jar. Half fill the jar with water. Add a handful each of gravel, sand, and soil to the water. Mix well with a spoon. Let the jar stand until the next day. How did the sediments settle at the bottom of the jar? How is this similar to sediment settling at the bottom of a lake?

Different sediments form different sedimentary rocks. Look at the picture of sandstone. Sandstone is formed from sediments of sand. Different materials cement the sand together. The material that cements the sand gives sandstone its color. Sandstone may be red, brown, yellow, or white.

Limestone is a sedimentary rock formed from many materials in water. Some limestone is very fine. It contains the remains of very tiny plants and animals. Other limestone is rough and contains large pieces of shells. Chalk is a type of limestone. When you write with chalk, you might be using a rock made from the shells of animals that lived long ago.

Sandstone

Fine limestone

Limestone containing shells

— PLANTS AND ANIMALS FROM — LONG AGO

How are fossils formed?

Sometimes scientists find traces of plants and animals in sedimentary rocks. These traces are called **fossils** (fos'əlz). Some fossils are bones, footprints, or the bodies of animals from long ago.

Another type of fossil is formed when a plant or animal dies and is covered with sediment. As the sediment hardens, the body of the plant or animal decays. This leaves an empty space in the sediment where the plant or animal used to be. This empty space is a **mold fossil.**

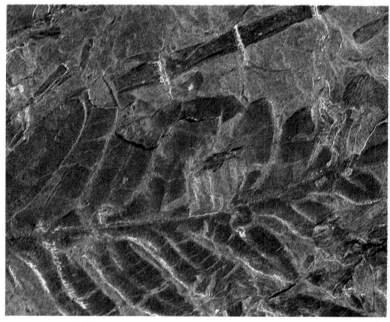

Mold fossils of ferns

Cast fossils of shells

Sometimes sediments or minerals may fill the mold. These materials may harden to form a cast fossil. The **cast fossil** is a rock with the exact shape of the original plant or animal. A cast fossil is like a gelatin mold. Gelatin hardens into the shape of the mold.

The trees you see in the picture are cast fossils. The trees are petrified (pet′rə fīd), or changed to rock. They formed when the buried trees began to rot. Minerals slowly took the place of the material in the trees. This formed the exact copy you see.

Petrified wood

189

Some plants that were buried long ago changed into coal. Coal is called a fossil fuel. Today we use this fuel for energy. The drawings show how coal forms. Gas and oil are other fossil fuels. They formed from layers of tiny dead animal matter. The animals lived in the sea long ago.

Plants and animals lived and died in large swamps.

Layers of dead plant matter built up over many years.

The swampy land sank and was covered with water and many layers of sediment.

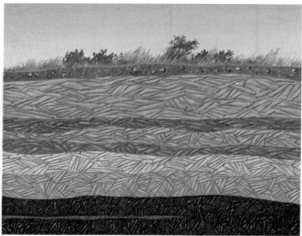

The heat and pressure of the sediments pressed down. After many years, coal was formed.

How do cast fossils and mold fossils form?

Materials   2 milk cartons / plaster of paris / plastic spoon / water / shells / petroleum jelly / scissors / hammer / hand lens

Procedure
A. Use scissors to cut off one side of a milk carton. Cut off the top of a second milk carton. Fill the second milk carton halfway with water. Slowly stir in plaster of paris until it is as thick as soft ice cream. Pour the plaster into the first carton.

B. Cover some shells with petroleum jelly. Press them halfway into the plaster. Let the plaster harden.

C. Remove the shells to see the imprints they made.
   1. What kind of fossil does this show?

D. Lightly cover the plaster and imprints with more petroleum jelly.

E. Mix more plaster to cover the imprints. Let the plaster harden.

F. Remove the milk carton. Use a hammer to break apart the two layers of plaster. Use the hand lens to compare the two fossils.
   2. What kind of fossil does this show?

Conclusion
1. How are the two fossils different?
2. Explain how each of these fossils form.

Shale changes to slate

ROCKS THAT CHANGE INTO OTHER ROCKS

How are metamorphic rocks formed?

Sometimes igneous and sedimentary rocks are buried deep in the earth. Great heat and pressure within the earth change the igneous and sedimentary rocks into a new kind of rock. This new kind of rock is called **metamorphic** (met ə môr'fik) **rock.**

Coal is one type of sedimentary rock that can be changed. Soft coal is a sedimentary rock. If soft coal is buried deep in the earth, heat and pressure may change it into hard coal. This metamorphic rock is much harder and is a better fuel than soft coal. More heat and pressure can cause the hard coal to form the mineral graphite. Graphite is not useful as a fuel. We use this mineral in making pencils. These pictures show examples of other metamorphic rocks.

Limestone changes to marble

Sandstone changes to quartzite

Granite changes to gneiss

Sandstone is a sedimentary rock that is easily scratched and broken. You can crush sandstone with a hammer. Heat and pressure change sandstone into quartzite (kwôrt′sīt). Quartzite is a metamorphic rock. Unlike sandstone, quartzite is very hard.

Limestone is a sedimentary rock that can change into marble. Marble is a very hard metamorphic rock used in buildings. Have you ever seen a marble building? Many of the buildings in Washington, D.C., are made of marble.

IDEAS TO REMEMBER

▶ The earth has a crust, a mantle, and a core.
▶ Minerals can be identified by testing their properties.
▶ Igneous rocks are formed from melted rock.
▶ Sedimentary rocks are formed from layers of sediment.
▶ Fossils show us what plants and animals from long ago looked like.
▶ Metamorphic rocks are formed from igneous and sedimentary rocks.

Reviewing the chapter

SCIENCE WORDS

A. Write the letter of the term that best matches the definition. Not all the terms will be used.

1. A trace of a plant or animal that lived long ago
2. The layer of the earth we live on
3. A pure solid material found in the ground
4. The middle layer of the earth
5. A rock formed from melted rock
6. The inner layer of the earth
7. A rock formed from sediment
8. A rock formed from other rocks that have been changed

   a. crust
   b. magma
   c. core
   d. metamorphic rock
   e. mineral
   f. fossil
   g. igneous rock
   h. mantle
   i. sedimentary rock
   j. sediment

B. Use science terms from the chapter to answer the questions.

1. I am the empty space in a sedimentary rock where a plant or animal once was. What am I?
2. I am the trace of an animal that lived long ago. Sediments and minerals filled the empty space where the animal once was. What am I?
3. I am melted rock within the earth. What am I?

UNDERSTANDING IDEAS

A. Match the description of the rock with its picture. Then tell whether the rock is an igneous rock, a sedimentary rock, or a metamorphic rock.

  1. A glassy rock formed when lava cools
  2. A rough rock formed when large pieces of shells are pressed together
  3. A light rock formed from lava that contained steam and gases

B. Describe three properties that can be used to identify a mineral. Give an example of a mineral for each property.

C. Metamorphic rocks are sometimes called ''changed rocks.'' In complete sentences, tell why this term can be used to describe metamorphic rocks.

USING IDEAS

1. Collect rocks in your neighborhood. Use reference books to identify them. Label the rocks. You can display your rock collection in a shoe box.

2. In your mind, create an animal that might have lived long ago. Make a drawing of a fossil from your animal.

Chapter 10

The Earth's Oceans

Smoke was rising from the ocean, but there was no burning ship to be seen. The people watched and wondered. Could it be a fire below the ocean's surface? The smoke became thicker and thicker as it filled the sky. Then suddenly fiery lava was thrown into the air. Great clouds of steam hissed as the hot lava touched the cold ocean water. A volcano was erupting from below the ocean's surface. When the eruptions stopped in June 1965, a new island, Surtsey, was formed near Iceland.

Surtsey is just one of many interesting things within the ocean. In this chapter you will learn what the earth's oceans are like and why they are important.

A LOOK AT THE OCEANS
What are the oceans like?

The oceans cover three fourths of the earth. If you look at the map, you can see just how large the oceans are. Can you move your finger around the world traveling only on the oceans? If you did, you showed that all the oceans are connected.

Have you ever tasted ocean water? If you have, you know it tastes salty. Has the ocean water always been salty? If not, where did the salt come from?

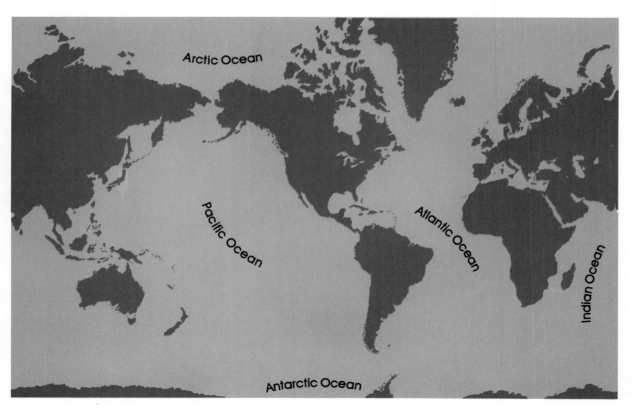

These drawings will help to show how the oceans became salty. Salt is one of many minerals found in the earth's crust. Rains washed salt from rocks and soil into streams and rivers. The streams and rivers then carried the salt to the ocean. In the ocean the salt was mixed with water. After many years the oceans became salty.

rain falling and soaking through soil

water dissolving minerals in the ground as it flows to rivers

The special submarine *Alvin*

rivers carrying minerals to the oceans

Scientists called oceanographers (ō shə-nog′rə fərs) have learned many things about the ocean. It is difficult to study the oceans because they are so large and deep. There is great pressure deep in the ocean. Oceanographers use special submarines to help them study the oceans. The special submarine shown above is named *Alvin. Alvin* has special cameras that scan the ocean floor and claws that it can use to collect samples.

THE OCEAN FLOOR

What is it like on the ocean floor?

Imagine taking a trip in *Alvin* along the ocean floor. As you begin your trip, you notice that the floor gently slopes down. It continues to slope for many kilometers. This area is called the **continental** (kon tə-nen′təl) **shelf.** The continental shelf is really the edge of the continent that is underwater. In some places the continental shelf is only 1 km wide. In other places it is as much as 800 km wide.

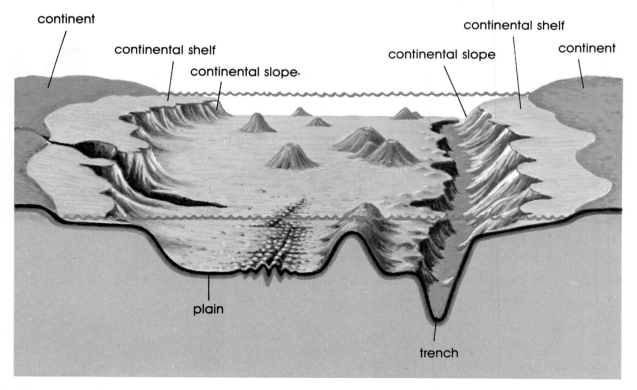

continent

continental shelf

continental slope

continental shelf

continental slope

continent

plain

trench

Hermit crab

The water on the continental shelf is shallow. Sunlight can reach the floor in many places. Many plants grow here. The plants are eaten by different types of fish. For this reason there is a great deal of fishing around the continental shelf. In these pictures you can see some of the types of living things found here.

As you continue your trip, you see that the ocean floor slopes more steeply. This steep drop is called the **continental slope.** There are deep canyons in the continental slope. Some of the canyons under the oceans are even larger than the Grand Canyon in Arizona.

Blue angelfish

Red East African starfish

201

When you reach the bottom of the continental slope, you are on the ocean floor **plain.** Here you can see hills, mountains, and valleys. Great mountain ranges rise from the ocean floor. Find the Mid-Atlantic Ridge on the map. The Mid-Atlantic Ridge is a very large chain of mountains on the bottom of the Atlantic Ocean. This chain of mountains is 16,000 km long. Some of the mountains are bigger than any mountains found on land. The tops of some of the mountains rise above the surface to form islands.

Mid-Atlantic Ridge

Some of the mountains are volcanoes. Lava builds up to make the volcanoes bigger after each eruption. Finally the tops of the volcanoes rise above the surface of the water to form islands. The Hawaiian Islands were formed in this way.

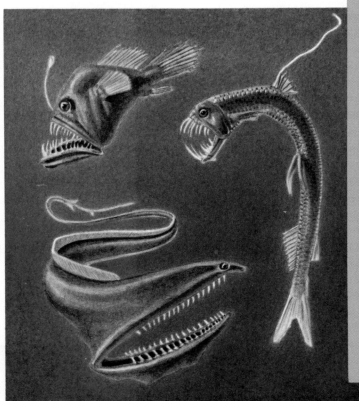

In some places you can see deep, narrow slits in the ocean floor. These slits are called **trenches.** The deepest trench in the world is the Mariana Trench in the Pacific Ocean. This trench is over 11 km deep.

As you continue your trip across the ocean floor, you reach another continental slope. This is an upward slope. Beyond it is another continental shelf. Finally you reach another continent to end your journey.

THE MOVING OCEAN

What are two ways we can see ocean water move?

Ocean water is always moving. Waves in the ocean show one kind of movement. Perhaps you have seen a surfer riding a large wave like the one in the picture. How did this wave form?

Most waves form far from the shore. These waves are formed by wind that blows across the surface of the ocean. Strong winds cause large waves to form. Some waves, formed by winds during storms, may be as high as a house.

Not all waves are formed by the wind. Some waves are caused by earthquakes in the bottom of the ocean. These earthquakes cause a giant wave to form. A giant wave formed by an earthquake is called a tsunami (tsü nä′mē). A tsunami can destroy whole towns as it crashes onto the shore.

Waves crash, or break, when they come close to shore. As you can see in the drawing, the top part of a wave is called the **crest.** The bottom part of a wave is called the **trough** (trôf). As a wave approaches shore, its trough drags on the ocean floor. This slows down the trough. At the same time, the crest keeps moving forward without slowing down. Soon the crest is in front of the trough. This makes the crest fall forward. The falling wave is called a **breaker.** The surfer on page 204 is riding on a breaker.

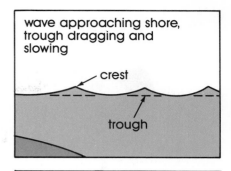

wave approaching shore, trough dragging and slowing

crest

trough

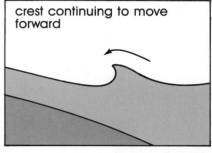

crest continuing to move forward

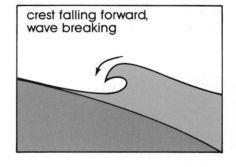

crest falling forward, wave breaking

Finding out

How does wind form waves? Fill a shallow pan halfway with water. Blow through a straw across the surface of the water to see how waves form. First blow softly. Slowly blow harder to see the difference in the waves. Observe the waves. Try to identify the crest and the trough.

Another way ocean water moves is by rising and falling. We can see the level of the ocean rise and fall along the shore. The level changes four times during a day. This change in the level of ocean water is called a **tide.**

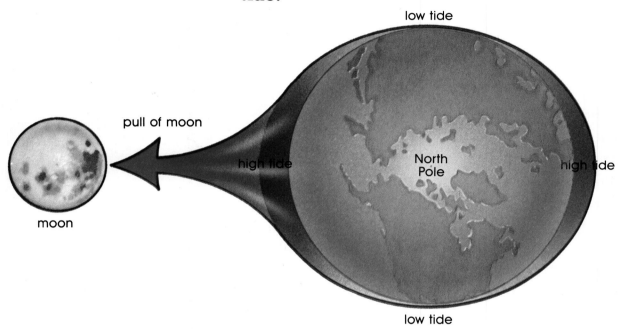

Finding out

What times are high tides and low tides?   Newspapers often print a tide chart like the one shown. Notice that the chart shows two high tides and two low tides for each day. If you were going fishing in the ocean, you would need to know the times of the tides. What time is the water deepest each day? If you were going to dig for clams, you would wait for low tide. What time is low tide each day?

TIDE TABLE			
	Tuesday	Wednesday	Thursday
Low Tide	1:49 A.M.	2:27 A.M.	3:03 A.M.
High Tide	7:55 A.M.	8:33 A.M.	9:10 A.M.
Low Tide	2:22 P.M.	3:02 P.M.	3:40 P.M.
High Tide	8:12 P.M.	8:50 P.M.	9:31 P.M.

High tide　　　　　　　　　　　　Low tide

Tides are caused mainly by the gravitational pull of the moon on the earth. The moon travels around the earth. The moon has a stronger pull on the side of the earth it is facing. The arrow in the drawing on page 206 shows the side of the earth that is being pulled most. The gravity of the moon pulls water to this side. The pull causes water on this side to rise. The rise in the water level is called **high tide.** In other places the water has been pulled away. This drop in water level is called **low tide.** Water on the other side of the earth is not pulled away by the moon. Therefore it stays at high tide. The spinning of the earth on its axis causes the tides to change. Each day there are two high tides and two low tides.

On rocky shorelines the high tide leaves behind pools of water. These tide pools are homes for many kinds of plants and animals. Crabs, starfish, and algae can be found in tide pools.

Tide pools

Living things in a tide pool

THE OCEAN'S RIVERS
What is a third way ocean water moves?

Did you know that there are large moving rivers of water in the ocean? These large ocean rivers are called **currents** (ker'ənts). Some of the currents are warm, while other currents are cold. Warm-water currents flow away from the equator. Cold-water currents carry cold water away from the North Pole and the South Pole. The arrows on the map show the path of some ocean currents. What types of currents affect the coastlines of North America?

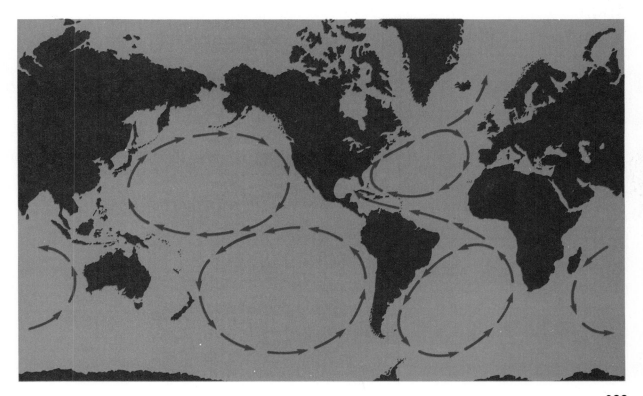

Look at the map of the Gulf Stream. The Gulf Stream is one of the strongest ocean currents on earth. The Gulf Stream is about 160 km wide and travels about 5 km per hour (km/h). The Gulf Stream carries warm water north from the equator. Many fish and plants live in the warm water of the Gulf Stream. Many people depend on these fish for food.

Notice on the map how the Gulf Stream moves along the east coast of North America. Land sometimes blocks ocean currents. When this happens, the path of the current changes. This causes the Gulf Stream to travel along the edge of North America. The spinning of the earth then causes the Gulf Stream to move toward Europe.

What happens when hot water meets cold water?

Materials   aquarium / blue food coloring / small plastic bottle with a hole in its lid / hot water / cold water

Procedure
A. Fill an aquarium with cold water.

B. Half fill a small plastic bottle with hot water. Add a few drops of blue food coloring. Then fill the bottle the rest of the way with more hot water. Cover the bottle with a lid that has a hole in it.
   1. Predict what will happen when the bottle is placed in the cold water.

C. Hold your finger over the hole in the lid. Place the bottle on the bottom of the aquarium. Slowly remove your hand from the water.
   2. Does a current form?
   3. Make a drawing to show what happens.

Conclusion
1. What happens when hot water meets cold water?
2. The Gulf Stream is a warm-water current. Do you think it flows near the surface or near the bottom of the ocean? Why?

Using science ideas
What happens when cold water meets warm water? Freeze an ice-cube tray filled with water and food coloring. Drop a colored ice cube into a clear container of warm water. Does a current form? How does it flow?

OCEAN RESOURCES

How are the oceans important to us?

People have sailed on the oceans for hundreds of years. Transportation is still one important way people use the oceans. Can you name some other ways people use them?

One way we use the oceans is for their resources (ri sôr′siz). A **resource** is a useful material taken from the earth. Minerals are resources found in the oceans. Some minerals are found in small black rocks on the ocean floor. These rocks are called **nodules** (noj′ülz). Nodules contain minerals such as copper and nickel.

Harbor

Fishing boat

Food from the sea is also an important resource. People eat fish and also feed fish to livestock. Seaweed has many uses. Did you know that seaweed is used to make some types of ice cream, candy, and medicines?

Natural gas and oil are resources that can be found beneath the ocean floor. As our oil and natural gas supplies on land are used up, we will need the oil and gas under the oceans.

The tides can be used to produce energy. This is called tidal power. The rise and fall of the water supplies the energy to make electricity. There is a tidal power plant in Seattle, Washington, that produces electricity. Someday tidal power may be a common energy source along the shores.

Offshore oil well

How can salt be removed from salt water?

Materials   warm water / salt / paper cup / plastic spoon / shallow dish

Procedure

A. Pour some warm water into a paper cup. Slowly stir in a spoonful of salt. Keep stirring to dissolve the salt.

B. Pour the salt water into a shallow dish. Place the dish in a warm place, like near a sunny window or on a radiator.

  1. What do you think will happen? Why?

C. Make a chart with headings, like the one shown.

D. Observe the dish each day until all the water has dried up. Write down the date and your observations on the chart.

  2. What was left in the dish after the water dried up?

  3. How long did it take for the water to dry up?

Conclusion

1. Use the chart to explain what happened to the water in the dish every day. Did the results you expected actually happen?
2. Explain how you removed the salt from the salt water.

Using science ideas

Put some salt water in another shallow dish. Think of a way to collect fresh water from the salt water. How could this be a useful thing to do?

Day	Description of salt water in dish

IDEAS TO REMEMBER

▶ Three fourths of the earth is covered by water.

▶ Ocean water contains dissolved salt and other minerals.

▶ Ocean water is always moving in waves, currents, or tides.

▶ The bottom of the ocean is covered by hills, valleys, mountains, and canyons.

▶ The oceans contain valuable resources, such as oil, natural gas, and minerals.

Reviewing the Chapter

SCIENCE WORDS

A. Copy the sentences below. Use science terms from the chapter to complete the sentences.

1. The steep drop in the ocean floor after the continental shelf is called the ____.
2. The top part of a wave is called the ____.
3. The bottom part of a wave is called the ____.
4. Black rocks on the ocean floor, called ____, contain many minerals.

B. Write the letter of the term that best matches the definition. Not all the terms will be used.

1. A rise in ocean water level
2. A river of water in the ocean
3. A useful material taken from the earth
4. The bottom of the ocean floor
5. The edge of a continent that is underwater
6. A fall in ocean water level
7. A deep, narrow slit in the ocean floor
8. A falling wave
9. A change in the level of ocean water

a. tide
b. low tide
c. breaker
d. *Alvin*
e. oceanographer
f. continental shelf
g. trench
h. high tide
i. plain
j. current
k. resource

UNDERSTANDING IDEAS

A. Copy the following groups of terms. Cross out the term that does not belong in each group. Then describe what the remaining terms have in common.

   1. plain, high tide, continental slope, trench
   2. nodules, tide, current, wave
   3. breaker, trough, resource, crest
   4. fish, minerals, natural gas, plain

B. Make a chart with headings like the one below. Using information from the chapter, list the ocean's resources in the first column. In the second column, tell how each resource is important. Then, in complete sentences, tell what would happen if every ocean resource was suddenly used up.

Resource	How resource is important

USING IDEAS

1. Find a map of the world in a reference book. Trace the map. Draw the ocean currents on your map. Show how two of the currents affect the lands they touch.

Chapter 11

Measuring Weather

What is the weather like today? Is it raining? Is it warm? Is it cold? Is it windy? These questions might be your first thoughts each day. Weather is important in your life. How you dress, what you do, and where you go depend on the weather. You may even find that different kinds of weather make you feel happy or sad.

It is hard to know for sure what the weather will be on a certain day. Observing weather every day helps you to tell what the weather is likely to be. In this chapter you will learn how weather conditions can be measured.

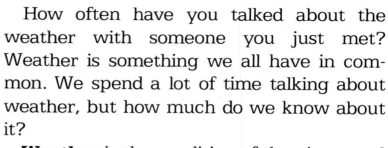

What is weather?

Foggy weather

How often have you talked about the weather with someone you just met? Weather is something we all have in common. We spend a lot of time talking about weather, but how much do we know about it?

Weather is the condition of the air around us. Changes in the condition of the air give us many types of weather. How many different types of weather can you name? You might remember a foggy night, a cold morning, or a windy day. The words *foggy, cold,* and *windy* describe the condition of the air.

Rainy weather

Snowy weather

Sunny weather

People say, "Don't count on the weather." But one thing about the weather we can count on is that it always changes. The weather may change from day to day and even from hour to hour. It may rain on one side of a city but not on the other side. When we talk about weather, we are talking about what is happening in the air in one place at one time.

Windy weather

221

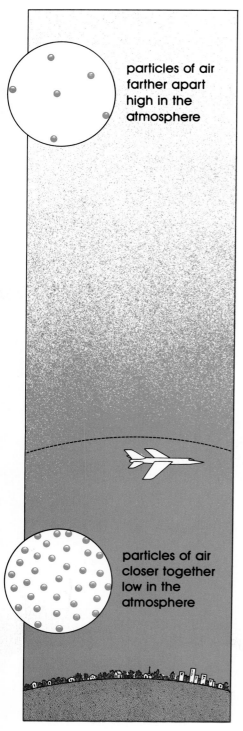

particles of air farther apart high in the atmosphere

particles of air closer together low in the atmosphere

The air that surrounds the earth is called the **atmosphere** (at'mə sfir). The atmosphere is about 2,500 km thick. There are four layers in the atmosphere.

The layer closest to the earth is the troposphere (trō'pə sfir). The troposphere is between 6 km and 16 km thick. Most of the air in the atmosphere is found here. The particles of air are packed close together in the troposphere. The air particles move farther apart as you go higher in the troposphere. The air is so thin in the upper layers of the troposphere that you would have trouble breathing. Often people who climb high mountains take a supply of oxygen with them.

The air also becomes colder as you go up in the troposphere. This is why many mountaintops are snow-covered even in the summer. The air outside a high-flying jet is about −40°C.

The troposphere is important because we breathe its air. All living things depend on water vapor in the troposphere. This is also where clouds, storms, and winds form.

You know that the weather changes from place to place and from day to day. By observing temperature, wind speed and direction, air pressure, and moisture, you can predict changes in the weather.

– CHANGES IN AIR TEMPERATURE –
How does air temperature change?

It takes a lot of energy to heat the air in the troposphere. Where do you think this energy comes from? Look at the drawing. Energy from the sun warms the surface of the earth. Heat from the surface of the earth then warms the air above. How does this help explain colder temperatures in the upper troposphere?

The surface of the earth does not heat evenly. During the day, air warms more quickly over land. At the same time, air warms more slowly over water. These differences in heating the earth's surface cause changes in air temperature. The changes in temperature cause weather changes.

heat

light

light

light

heat

heat

sun slowly warming water

water slowly warming air above it

sun quickly warming land

land quickly warming air above it

Thermometer

Temperature is measured with a thermometer. Most thermometers are made of a glass tube with colored alcohol inside. When the air gets hotter, the level of the liquid in the tube rises. When the air cools, the liquid level falls.

Look at the picture of the thermometer. The scale on the left side of this thermometer measures temperature in degrees Celsius. The temperature of your classroom is about 20°C. What temperature does this thermometer show? What would you wear if this was the temperature outside?

Do you know?

Have you ever looked at a thermometer outside, and then found that you felt much colder than you thought you would? Chances are that the weather was windy. The wind can make you feel colder than the air around you. This cooling effect is called wind chill.

If the air temperature is 10°C, a wind blowing 32 km/h will make you feel like it is 0°C. Look at the table. How cold will the air feel if the temperature is 4°C and the wind blows at 16 km/h?

WINDCHILL CHART

Wind speed (km/h)	Thermometer reading (°C)						
	10	4	−1	−6	−12	−17	−23
Calm	10	4	−1	−6	−12	−17	−23
8	8	2	−2	−8	−14	−20	−26
16	4	−2	−8	−15	−22	−29	−36
24	2	−5	−12	−20	−27	−38	−43
32	0	−7	−15	−23	−32	−39	−46
40	−1	−8	−17	−26	−34	−42	−50
48	−2	−10	−18	−27	−36	−44	−53
56	−2.5	−11	−20	−28	−37	−45	−54
64	−3	−12	−21	−29	−39	−46	−56

TEMPERATURES FOR OCTOBER 16

Time	Temperature
4 A.M.	6°C
8 A.M.	8°C
12 A.M.	16°C
4 P.M.	14°C
8 P.M.	11°C
12 P.M.	9°C

8 A.M.

12 A.M.

4 P.M.

The temperature of the air is always changing. Within a single day, temperatures may differ from hour to hour. By using a thermometer you can keep a record of these changes. Look at this daily temperature chart. On what day were these temperatures recorded? At what time of the day was it the warmest? The coldest? What was the air temperature at 8 A.M.? What do you think caused these differences in temperature?

Air temperature is a very important part of the weather. If the temperature of the air never changed, the weather would always be the same. A change in temperature causes changes in air pressure, wind, and the amount of moisture in the air.

AIR PRESSURE

How does air press on the earth?

Have you ever felt your ears "pop" when you rode in a car driving up a mountain road? If you have, you felt a change in **air pressure.** You might also have felt this change while riding in an elevator or flying in an airplane.

It might be difficult to think of air having pressure at all, but it does. All the air in the atmosphere pushes down on everything on earth. When you climb a mountain, you are going higher into the atmosphere. There is less air above you, so there is less air pressure.

Low-pressure area

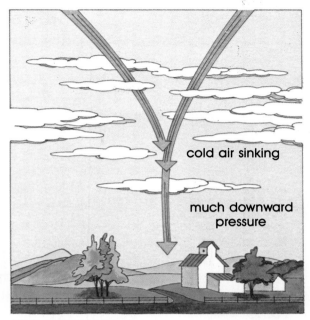

High-pressure area

The air pressure at the surface of the earth does not stay the same. When a part of the earth is heated, the air above it gets warmer. The warm air begins to rise. As it rises, it does not press downward as much on the earth's surface. This results in less pressure on the earth. This warm rising air forms a **low-pressure area.** It is called a *low* on a weather map.

The rising warm air cools slowly. As the air cools, it becomes heavier. In time it sinks to the earth's surface. The sinking air puts more pressure on the earth. This cool air forms a **high-pressure area.** It is called this because there is more downward pressure by air. It is called a *high* on the weather map.

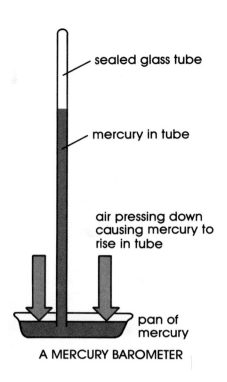

sealed glass tube

mercury in tube

air pressing down
causing mercury to
rise in tube

pan of
mercury

A MERCURY BAROMETER

Changes in air pressure can be measured with a **barometer** (bə rom'ə tər). In the drawing you can see one kind of barometer, called a mercury barometer. A mercury barometer consists of a glass tube that has one end sealed. There is very little air in the closed end of the tube. The tube is partly filled with mercury. Its open end sits in a pan of mercury. Air pushes down on the mercury in the pan. This pushes the mercury up the tube. When air pressure increases, more air pushes on the pan of mercury. This causes the mercury level to rise in the tube. When air pressure decreases, less air pushes on the pan of mercury. This causes the mercury level to fall in the tube. By measuring the height of the mercury in the tube, you can measure the air pressure.

Finding out

How can you measure air pressure?   Make a barometer with a wide-mouth jar, a large balloon, rubber bands, a drinking straw, and glue. Cut a large piece from the balloon. Stretch it over the mouth of the jar. Use one or two rubber bands to hold the balloon in place. Glue the straw to the lid for a pointer.

Tape a piece of paper to the wall. Place your barometer next to the paper. Mark a line where the straw is pointing. Write down the day and the weather conditions. Do this every day for a week. Then see if you can use your barometer to predict the weather.

Another type of barometer consists of a metal box that has had some air removed. The box is attached to a pointer on a dial. Air pressure pushes on the sides of the box. This pressure causes the pointer to move to a higher number on the dial. When air pressure decreases, the pointer moves back to a lower number.

A barometer can help you to predict the weather. A slowly rising pressure may mean fair weather. A steady pressure means the weather will stay the same. A slowly falling pressure indicates stormy weather. The barometer shown below has a description of the weather on its dial. What type of weather is the pointer indicating?

Barometer

— WIND SPEED AND DIRECTION —
How does wind move?

It has often been said that the wind brings us our weather. Wind is the movement of air. As air moves, it brings warmth, cold, rain, or snow. Differences of temperature and pressure cause air to move.

During the day, the surface of the earth heats up. It heats up faster in some areas than it does in others. Beaches, highways, and buildings heat up quickly. Forests, grassy fields, and bodies of water heat up slowly. When warm air rises, cooler air moves in to take its place. For example, the warm air over a road rises. Cooler air over a nearby field moves under the rising warm air. The cooler air then starts to heat up quickly. What happens to this air as it becomes warmer?

warm air rising

cooler air moving down

Wind vane

Knowing the speed and direction of the wind can be a great help in predicting the weather. Have you ever seen a wind vane on the roof of a house? Wind vanes show the direction of the wind. The arrow of the vane points into the wind. When wind is blowing from the south, it is called a south wind. What would you call a wind blowing from west to east? Sometimes the arrow of the vane points between two directions. When the arrow points between the north and the west, it is called a northwest wind. Look at the wind vane in the picture. From what direction is the wind blowing?

Anemometer

An instrument that measures how fast the wind is moving is an **anemometer** (an ə-mom'ə tər). Look at the picture of the anemometer. The wind causes the cups to spin. The speed of the cups is recorded in kilometers per hour. Before anemometers were used, people judged wind speed by how wind moved the objects around them. A scale showing different wind speeds is shown below. The scale is called the Beaufort scale. Use this scale to tell what the wind speed is outside your school today.

BEAUFORT WIND SCALE

	Description of wind	Type of wind	Wind speed (km/h)		Description of wind	Type of wind	Wind speed (km/h)
	Smoke rising straight up	Calm	0.0– 0.7		Loose paper blown	Moderate breeze	20.0–28.5
	Smoke drifting	Light air	0.8– 5.4		Small trees swaying	Fresh breeze	29.0–38.5
	Wind felt on face; wind vane moving	Light breeze	5.5–12.0		Umbrella difficult to control	Strong wind	39.0–50.0
	Flags blown straight out	Gentle breeze	12.1–19.5		Difficult to walk	Stiff wind	50.5–61.5

How does an anemometer measure wind speed?

Materials 4 small paper cups / tape / 4 plastic drinking straws / stapler / straight pin with a large head / pencil with a new eraser

Procedure

A. To make an anemometer, staple one end of a plastic drinking straw to the side of a paper cup near its open end. Repeat this with three other straws and cups. Make sure that all the straws are stapled to the same side of the cup.

B. Set two of the cups on their sides so that the straws are on top. Arrange the two cups so the ends of the straws are alongside each other, as shown. Tape the two straws together. Repeat this with the two other cups and straws.

C. Lay the two pairs of straws across each other to form a cross. Tape the two pairs of straws together.

D. Carefully push a straight pin through the center of the cross and into the top of a new pencil eraser. Try blowing on the anemometer you have made to make it spin.

E. Take your anemometer outside. Count how many times it spins in 1 minute.

   1. How many times does it spin in 1 minute?

Conclusion
How does an anemometer measure wind speed?

Using science ideas
How does measuring wind speed help us to predict weather?

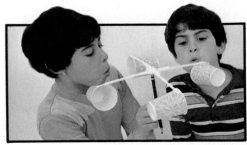

233

WATER IN THE AIR
How do clouds form?

Have you ever wondered why water is found in so many places? As you can see in the drawing, water from oceans, lakes, and rivers gets heated by the sun. As the water heats up, some of it escapes into the air as gas. This gas is called **water vapor.**

When the air has a large amount of water vapor, tiny droplets start to form. Countless numbers of these droplets make up clouds. As the air in a cloud cools, the tiny droplets come closer together. Small droplets come together to form bigger droplets. These fall to the ground as rain, sleet, or snow. When water falls to the ground, it is called **precipitation** (pri sip ə tā'shən). This water moves to oceans, lakes, and rivers.

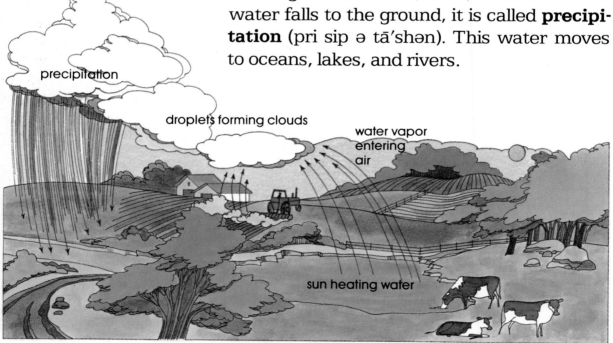

precipitation

droplets forming clouds

water vapor entering air

sun heating water

How does the weather change during the week?

Materials thermometer

Procedure

A. Make a chart like the one shown.

B. Write down today's date in the first column.

C. Use a thermometer to measure the temperature outside. Write this number in the second column.

D. Describe today's cloud cover in the third column. If there are no clouds, write *Clear.* If the sky is completely filled with clouds, write *Cloudy.* If some sky can be seen through the clouds, write *Partly cloudy.*

E. Using the wind chart on page 232, determine the wind speed. Write the wind speed in the fourth column.

F. Describe today's weather in the fifth column. You might use words such as *Fair, Raining, Snowing, Windy, Cold,* or *Hot.*

G. Repeat steps **B** through **F** at the same time every day for 1 week.

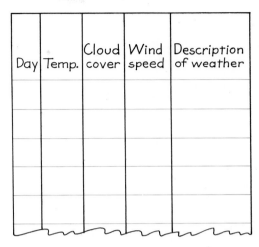

Day	Temp.	Cloud cover	Wind speed	Description of weather

Conclusion

1. What day had the highest temperature? What day had the lowest?

2. How many days were clear? How many were partly cloudy? How many were cloudy?

3. What was the wind speed on the windiest day? What was it on the calmest day?

4. In general, how did the weather change during the week?

Precipitation is measured with a rain gauge such as the one shown here. During a rainstorm, rain falls into the tube. Rainfall is measured in inches (in.). On this rain gauge the inches scale is on the right. How many inches of water are in this rain gauge?

Snow can also be collected in a rain gauge. Scientists have found that 10 in. of snow has the same amount of water as 1 in. of rain.

Most of the moisture in the atmosphere cannot be seen. Even when the sky is cloudless, the air still holds water. Warm air can hold more water vapor than cold air. The amount of water the air holds is called **humidity** (hyü mid′ə tē). This picture shows a hot summer day. On days such as this, the air may have a lot of water vapor in it. The weather is said to be humid. How do people feel on a hot humid day?

Rain gauge

An instrument used to measure humidity is a **hygrometer** (hī grom'ə tər). The hygrometer shown here consists of two thermometers. The bulb of the thermometer on the right is covered with a wet cloth. The temperature on this thermometer is lower than the temperature on the other thermometer. Humidity is measured by comparing the two temperatures and using a chart.

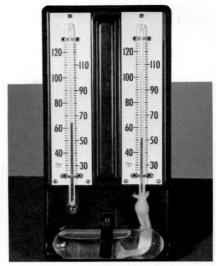

Hygrometer

IDEAS TO REMEMBER

► Weather is the condition of the air in one place at one time. Weather occurs in the troposphere.

► Temperature, wind speed and direction, air pressure, and moisture can be measured to predict the weather.

► Air temperature is measured with a thermometer.

► A barometer can measure air pressure to predict the weather.

► A wind vane shows wind direction; an anemometer measures wind speed.

► Water that falls to earth is called precipitation.

► Humidity is the amount of water the air holds. It is measured by a hygrometer.

Reviewing the Chapter

SCIENCE WORDS

A. Write the letter of the term that best matches the definition. Not all the terms will be used.

1. An instrument that measures air pressure
2. An area of warm rising air
3. Any water that falls to the ground
4. The air surrounding the earth
5. Water in the air
6. An instrument that measures wind speed
7. The condition of the air around us

a. atmosphere
b. anemometer
c. weather
d. low-pressure area
e. barometer
f. high-pressure area
g. precipitation
h. humidity

B. Copy the sentences below. Use science terms from the chapter to complete each sentence.

1. An instrument that measures humidity is a/an ____.
2. The force of the air pushing down on everything on earth is called ____.
3. An area of cooled heavy air is called a/an ____.
4. Water that escapes into the air as a gas is called ____.

UNDERSTANDING IDEAS

A. Describe the troposphere. Tell why it is so important.

B. Identify each of the following instruments. Explain how each instrument is used.

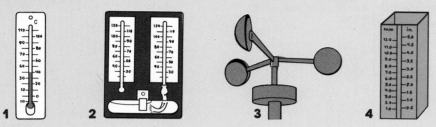

C. Tell which of the following sentences are true and which are false.

1. Weather is always changing.
2. By observing temperature, wind speed and direction, air pressure, and moisture, you can predict changes in the weather.
3. The earth's surface is heated evenly.
4. The temperature of the air always stays the same.
5. Warm air can hold more moisture than cold air can.

USING IDEAS

1. Set up a weather station outside your home. Use the barometer you made on page 228, the anemometer you made on page 233, and a thermometer. Keep a daily record of the weather for a month.

Chapter 12

The Solar System

Can you imagine what our solar system would look like to explorers from deep in outer space? They would find a family of planets unlike any other. They would also find billions of smaller objects.

After studying each planet they would learn that some planets are very hot, while others are very cold. They would learn that some planets are made mainly of gas, while others are made mainly of rock. The explorers would find out that each planet is different from the others.

In this chapter you, too, will study our sun and its family. You will learn about the planets and the billions of smaller objects that make up our solar system.

View of Saturn from Voyager 2

—— THE SUN AND ITS FAMILY ——
Which planets are inner planets and which are outer planets?

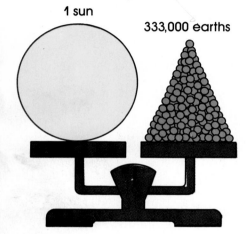

1 sun

333,000 earths

For thousands of years people have wondered what the sun was. Some thought the sun was a ball of fire. Others thought it was some sort of god slowly riding across the sky.

Today scientists know that the sun is a huge ball of hot churning gases. They have learned that it is a million times larger than the earth. They know that it is hundreds of thousands of times heavier than the earth. They also know that the sun gives off huge amounts of energy. A small part of this energy reaches the earth about 8 minutes after it leaves the sun.

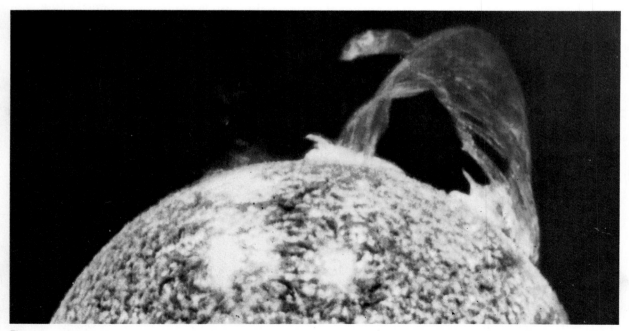

The sun

Nine planets revolve, or travel around, the sun. The time it takes for a planet to revolve around the sun is called a year. An Earth year is 365 days long. The farther a planet is from the sun, the longer its year is. A year on the planet closest to the sun is 88 Earth days long. A year on the planet farthest from the sun is 247 Earth years long.

Each planet also rotates, or spins on its axis. The time it takes for a planet to rotate once is called a day. An Earth day is 24 hours long. A day on the planet with the shortest day is less than 10 Earth hours long. A day on the planet with the longest day is about 176 Earth days long.

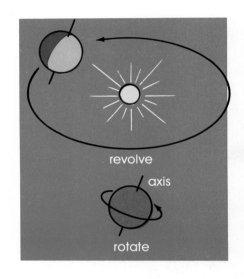

revolve

axis

rotate

Finding out

What does an ellipse look like? The path that planets follow as they revolve around the sun is called an ellipse (i lips'). To draw an ellipse, tape some paper to a bulletin board. The paper should be about 60 cm long and 45 cm wide. Insert two pushpins near the center of the paper. The pushpins should be 14 cm apart. Tie the end of a string together to make a loop. The loop should be 30 cm long. Place the loop around both pins.

Hold a pencil against the inside of the loop. Use the pencil to pull the loop tight. Guide the pencil around the inside of the loop until you reach the point at which you started. The shape you have drawn is an ellipse.

The nine planets can be divided into two groups. The four planets closest to the sun can be called the **inner planets.** Mercury (mėr′kyər ē), Venus (vē′nəs), Earth, and Mars are the inner planets. The five planets farthest from the sun can be called the **outer planets.** Jupiter (jü′pə tər), Saturn (sat′ərn), Uranus (yur′ə nəs), Neptune (nep′tün), and Pluto (plü′tō) are the outer planets.

Look at the drawing of the solar system. What ways can you see that the inner planets are different from the outer planets?

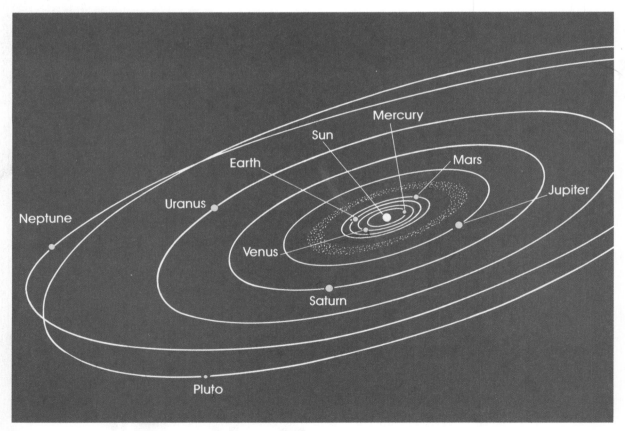

What does a model of the solar system look like?

Materials   tape / meterstick / paper models of the planets and the sun

Procedure
A. Get paper models of the planets and the sun from your teacher. Tape the model of the sun to the wall at one end of a hallway.

B. Measure 58 mm from this sun. Tape the model of Mercury at this point.
   1. If Mercury is this far from the sun in this model, at what point in the hallway do you think Pluto will be?

C. Measure 50 mm from Mercury. Tape the model of Venus at this point. Tape the model of Earth 42 mm from Venus. Tape the model of Mars 78 mm from Earth.

D. Measure 55.1 <u>cm</u> from Mars. Tape the model of Jupiter at this point. Tape the model of Saturn 65.1 cm from Jupiter. Tape the model of Uranus 144 cm from Saturn. Tape the model of Neptune 163 cm from Uranus. Tape the model of Pluto 140 cm from Neptune.
   2. How close is Pluto to where you thought it would be?

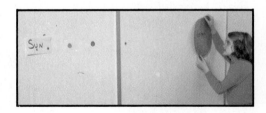

Conclusion
1. How would you describe the location of the planets in your model of the solar system?
2. How do the distances between the inner planets compare to the distances between the outer planets?

THE INNER PLANETS

How are the inner planets different from each other?

The planet closest to the sun is **Mercury.** Mercury is the fastest-moving planet in the solar system. It takes only 88 Earth days for Mercury to complete one trip around the sun. Mercury is also a very hot planet. In the daytime, temperatures can reach 425°C.

Mercury is a little larger than our moon. Look at the drawing of the surface of Mercury. How is this surface like the surface of the moon?

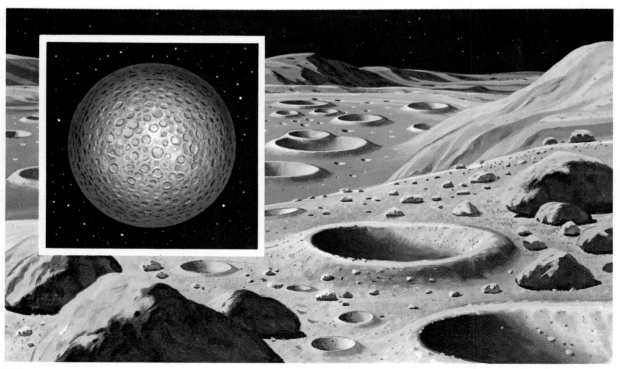

Mercury

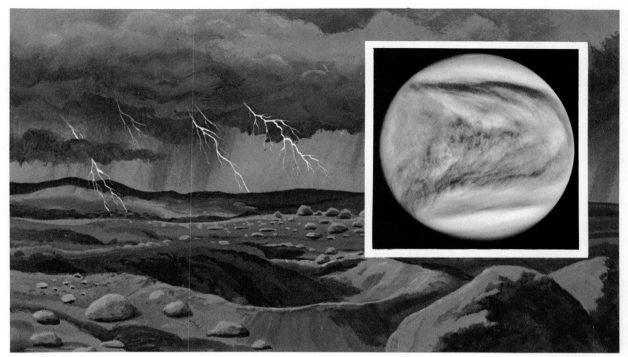

Venus

The second planet from the sun is **Venus.** Venus is about the same size as Earth. It is also the closest planet to Earth. Like Earth, Venus has an atmosphere. But the atmosphere of Venus is very dense. The upper atmosphere has layers of thick clouds. The lower atmosphere is mainly carbon dioxide gas. The dense atmosphere helps to keep the temperature on the surface at about 450°C. The atmosphere presses down with a force that is 90 times greater than air pressure on Earth.

Venus only rotates twice for every trip around the sun. So every year on Venus is about two days long!

Earth

Our planet, **Earth,** is the third planet from the sun. From space, our planet looks like a blue ball covered by swirling clouds. The atmosphere of Earth is made mainly of nitrogen, oxygen, and carbon dioxide. Water covers about three fourths of the surface of our planet. The temperature at the surface rarely goes below −30°C or above 43°C.

Unlike Mercury or Venus, Earth has a moon. The moon revolves around Earth about once every 27 days. The moon is about one-fourth the size of Earth. Besides having a moon, in what other ways is Earth different from Mercury and Venus?

The fourth planet from the sun is **Mars.** For hundreds of years people thought life could be found on Mars. Large lines that could be seen on the planet were thought to be canals. When the planet was explored, however, no signs of life were found.

Mars is like Earth in many ways. In the summer, daytime temperatures on Mars can reach 27°C. Both planets rotate at about the same rate. Also, small amounts of frozen water can be found on Mars. Unlike Earth, Mars has two moons. Both of these moons are much smaller than our moon. As you can see in this picture, Mars appears red. The color is caused by a rustlike dust on the surface. This dust is blown around by winds on Mars. Mars was named after the Roman god of war. Can you guess why?

Mars

You can use the following table to compare the inner planets. You can also use the drawings below the table to compare the sizes of the inner planets. Which planet is the smallest? Which has the longest day? Which has the shortest year? How much farther from the sun is Mars than Mercury? How much longer is a year on Earth than a year on Venus?

THE INNER PLANETS

Planet	Average distance from sun (in millions of km)	Diameter (in km)	Length of year (in Earth time)	Length of day (in Earth time)	Number of known moons
Mercury	58	4,880	88 days	176 days	0
Venus	108	12,100	225 days	116.7 days	0
Earth	150	12,756	365 days	24 hours	1
Mars	228	6,784	687 days	24.6 hours	2

Mercury

Venus

Earth

Mars

THE OUTER PLANETS

How do the outer planets differ?

Beyond Mars lies the fifth planet, **Jupiter.** Jupiter is the largest planet in the solar system. About 1,000 Earths could fill the inside of this giant planet. Jupiter is so large that it has its own family of moons. At least 16 moons revolve around Jupiter. One of Jupiter's moons has active volcanoes on it. Ice can be found on another. One of Jupiter's moons can be seen in front of the planet in the larger picture below.

Unlike any of the inner planets, Jupiter is made almost completely of gases. Huge storms move through these gases. The largest of these storms forms the Great Red Spot, which you can see in the smaller picture below. This one storm is as big as three Earths! Jupiter also has a ring that is thought to be made of rocky materials.

Jupiter

Saturn

The sixth planet from the sun is **Saturn.** Saturn is the second largest planet in the solar system. Like Jupiter, Saturn is made mainly of gases. And like Jupiter, Saturn has a large family of moons. At least 21 moons revolve around Saturn.

Saturn is best known for its beautiful rings. These rings can easily be seen from Earth with a telescope. Scientists have learned that Saturn's six large rings are made up of hundreds of smaller rings. Each smaller ring seems to be made of millions of frozen particles.

The seventh planet, **Uranus,** takes 84 Earth years to travel around the sun. While making this trip, Uranus rotates on its side. If people lived at the north pole of Uranus, they would have a night that would last 42 Earth years! This night would be followed by a day just as long. Can you imagine what a day that is 42 years long would be like?

Like Jupiter and Saturn, Uranus is made mainly of gas. Scientists think the atmosphere is made of hydrogen and helium. Uranus also has about nine rings and about five moons.

The smallest of the gaseous planets is **Neptune.** Neptune is about the same size and color as Uranus. But unlike Uranus, Neptune does not rotate on its side.

Neptune has two moons. The smaller of the two moons takes 1 Earth year to make a trip around Neptune. The larger moon is much closer to Neptune. This moon takes only 6 Earth days to revolve once. This larger moon makes the trip backwards!

Uranus

Neptune

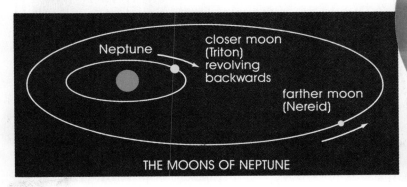

Neptune

closer moon
(Triton)
revolving
backwards

farther moon
(Nereid)

THE MOONS OF NEPTUNE

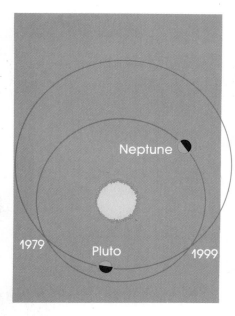

Until 1999, **Pluto** is the eighth planet. As you can see in the drawings, Pluto's orbit makes it the ninth planet from the sun for most of its year. Pluto takes longer than any other planet to revolve around the sun. Each trip takes 247 Earth years. From Pluto the sun looks like a bright star. The sun cannot warm this distant planet much. The temperature on Pluto stays around −230°C.

Unlike the other outer planets, Pluto is solid. Pluto is also the smallest planet in the solar system. It is about one-quarter the size of Earth. Pluto has one moon.

Pluto

THE OUTER PLANETS

Planet	Average distance from sun (in millions of km)	Diameter (in km)	Length of year (in Earth time)	Length of day (in Earth time)	Number of known moons
Jupiter	778	143,200	11.9 years	9.9 hours	16
Saturn	1,425	120,000	29.5 years	10.4 hours	21
Uranus	2,867	51,400	84 years	16 hours	5
Neptune	4,497	49,500	164.1 years	18.5 hours	2
Pluto	5,900	3,000	247 years	6.4 days	1

This table and drawing describe the outer planets. Which of these planets is the largest? Which is the smallest? Compare the outer planets with the inner planets on page 250. How much longer is the day on Mercury than the day on Pluto?

What are conditions like on the other planets?

Procedure

A. Pretend that you are an astronaut preparing to explore the solar system. You have been given the chart below so that you can prepare for your trip.

1. On which planets could you land your spacecraft?
2. On which planets would you find the atmosphere different from Earth?
3. For which planets would you need to bring protection from heat?
4. On which planets would you find the gravity to be less than that on Earth?

B. Now pretend that you are in your spacecraft on the way to Mars.

5. What things would you need in your spacecraft to survive on Mars?

Conclusion

In general, how are conditions alike on the inner planets? On the outer planets?

OFFICIAL PLANET DATA

PLANET	AVERAGE TEMPERATURE	WHAT PLANET IS MAINLY MADE OF	AMOUNT OF GRAVITY COMPARED TO EARTH	GASES FOUND IN ATMOSPHERE
MERCURY	425 C	ROCK	LESS	VERY FEW, IF ANY, GASES
VENUS	450 C	ROCK	LESS	CARBON DIOXIDE
EARTH	15 C	ROCK	XXXX	NITROGEN, OXYGEN, WATER
MARS	12 C	ROCK	LESS	CARBON DIOXIDE, WATER
JUPITER	−130 C	GAS	GREATER	HYDROGEN, METHANE
SATURN	−180 C	GAS	LESS	HYDROGEN, METHANE
URANUS	−215 C	GAS	LESS	HYDROGEN, METHANE
NEPTUNE	−200 C	GAS	GREATER	HYDROGEN, METHANE
PLUTO	−250 C	ROCK	LESS	VERY FEW, IF ANY, GASES

-OTHER MEMBERS OF THE SOLAR - SYSTEM

What are asteroids, meteors, and comets?

Besides the sun, the planets, and the moons, there are many other members of our solar system. One group of objects are called comets (kom'its). A **comet** is a mass of frozen gas and dust. Like planets, comets revolve around the sun. But unlike planets, the orbit of a comet may be long and narrow. This orbit can bring a comet very close to the sun. Some comets pass by the sun every few years. Others may pass by only once every 100 years or more.

As a comet approaches the sun, its gases begin to heat up. As the gases heat up, they produce a long tail. The tail may be millions of kilometers long. It usually points away from the sun.

tail

head

Do you know?

One of the best-known and brightest comets is Halley's comet. Halley's comet was named after Edmund Halley. In 1700 Halley said the comets that people saw in 1531, 1607, and 1682 were all the same comet. Halley also predicted that the comet would return in 1758, which it did.

Halley's comet can be seen about once every 76 years. It was seen in 1910. When is the next time this comet might be seen?

A second group of objects are called asteroids (as'tə roidz). **Asteroids** are pieces of rock that orbit the sun between Mars and Jupiter. Some asteroids are small lumps of rock. Others are very large. The largest known asteroid is about 3,400 km across. It is a little smaller than the moon. Most asteroids take about 5 years to orbit the sun.

Besides asteroids, there are other pieces of rock in space. When one of these rocks is pulled into our atmosphere, it is called a **meteor** (mē′tē ər). Have you ever seen a "shooting star"? A shooting star is not a star. It is a meteor burning as it passes through the atmosphere. Sometimes a meteor strikes the ground. A meteor that strikes the ground is called a **meteorite** (mē′tē ə rīt). Very few meteorites are ever found. This is because most meteors completely burn up in the atmosphere.

A meteorite

IDEAS TO REMEMBER

▶ Our solar system is made up of a sun, nine planets, and moons. It also has countless smaller objects including comets and asteroids.

▶ The four inner planets are Mercury, Venus, Earth, and Mars.

▶ The five outer planets are Jupiter, Saturn, Uranus, Neptune, and Pluto.

▶ A belt of rocks called asteroids separates the inner planets from the outer planets.

▶ Comets are masses of gas and dust that revolve around the sun.

Reviewing the Chapter

SCIENCE WORDS

A. Use these terms to answer the questions.

asteroid   meteor   comet   meteorite

1. I am a piece of rock from space that has been pulled into Earth's atmosphere. What am I?
2. I am a piece of rock that orbits the sun between Mars and Jupiter. What am I?
3. I am a piece of rock from space that falls through Earth's atmosphere and strikes the ground. What am I?
4. I am a mass of frozen gas and dust. I have a head and a long tail. What am I?

B. Use all the terms below to complete the sentences.

Mars   inner planets   Neptune   Pluto
Uranus   outer planets   Jupiter   Saturn
Earth   Mercury   Venus

The solar system is made of nine planets. Our planet, __1__, is one of the four planets closest to the sun. This group of planets can be called the __2__. The other three planets in this group are __3__, __4__, and __5__. The five planets farthest from the sun can be called the __6__. Until 1999 the farthest of these planets is __7__ · The other planets in this group are __8__, __9__, __10__, and __11__.

UNDERSTANDING IDEAS

A. Write the letter of the planet that best matches the description. Not all the planets will be used.

1. It has daytime temperatures of 425°C. It takes 88 Earth days to rotate once.
2. It has one moon. Its surface is mainly covered with water.
3. It has two moons. Small amounts of frozen water can be found on its surface.
4. It has at least 21 moons and 6 large beautiful rings.

    a. Jupiter
    b. Neptune
    c. Mars
    d. Mercury
    e. Saturn
    f. Earth

B. Identify each of the following.

1   2   3   4

C. What is an asteroid? Where are asteroids found? How is an asteroid different from a comet?

USING IDEAS

A. Pretend you are an astronaut. You have discovered a tenth planet. Describe your trip to the planet and your experiences on it. Draw a picture of the surface of the planet.

Science in Careers

Earth science involves the study of the solid, liquid, and gaseous parts of the earth. There are many careers for people in earth science.

Meteorologist

Geologist

Geology is the study of the solid earth. Different geologists study different aspects of the earth. A *paleontologist* is a geologist who studies fossils. A *petroleum geologist* studies where oil is found. *Mineralogists* study minerals. A *volcanologist* is a geologist who studies volcanoes.

Oceanography is the study of the oceans. *Physical oceanographers* study ocean currents, tides, and waves. They also study underwater sound. *Chemical oceanographers* study the chemistry of salt water. *Biological oceanographers* study the living things in the sea. *Geological oceanographers* use echo sounders to map the ocean floor.

Meteorologists are scientists who study the atmosphere. They make measurements that help them predict weather. Many predictions are made with the help of computers.

People in Science

Linda A. Morabito (1953–   )

Linda Morabito is a navigation engineer. She is one of a team that helped to steer the space probe Voyager 1 past Jupiter.

On March 9, 1979, Morabito made an important discovery. She was checking a picture that Voyager 1 had taken of Io, one of Jupiter's moons. She used a computer to brighten the picture on a screen. Suddenly she spotted a large umbrella-shaped cloud on the edge of Io. This was the very first time that an active volcano had been seen anyplace but on Earth.

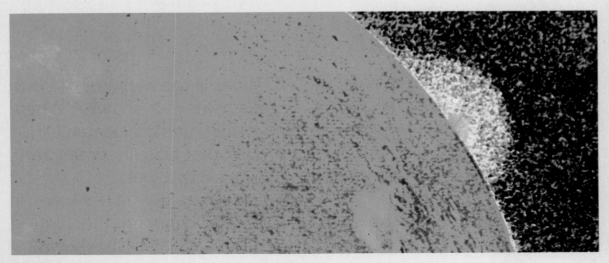

Volcano on Io

Developing Skills

WORD SKILLS

Many English words have word parts that come from other languages. This table lists some of these word parts. Use the table to help you write a definition for each of the words listed. You can do this by breaking each word into parts. For example, the word <u>atmosphere</u> is made of the parts <u>atmo-</u> and <u>sphere</u>. Check your definitions by looking in a dictionary.

1. atmosphere
2. geology
3. hydrosphere
4. lithosphere
5. telescope
6. topography

Word part	Meaning
atmo-	vapor, steam
geo-	earth
hydro-	water
litho-	stone
tele-	over a long distance
topo-	place
sphere	globe
-graphy	writing
-logy	science of
-scope	for seeing

READING A PICTOGRAPH

The graph on the next page is called a pictograph. A pictograph uses drawings or pictures to compare things. Use the pictograph to answer these questions.

1. What is the name of the highest waterfall shown?

2. What is the name of the lowest waterfall shown? Where is this waterfall located?
3. List the falls in order from highest to lowest.
4. What is the difference in height between the highest and the lowest falls shown?

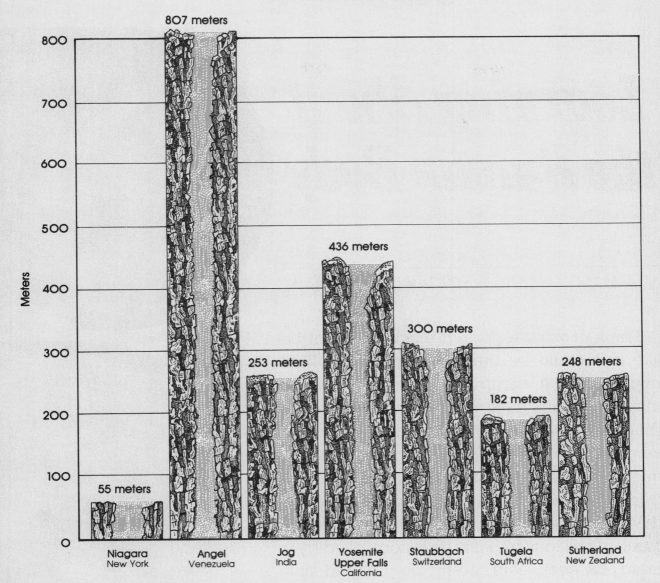

HEIGHTS OF MAJOR WATERFALLS

Meters

807 meters

436 meters

300 meters

253 meters

248 meters

182 meters

55 meters

Niagara
New York

Angel
Venezuela

Jog
India

Yosemite
Upper Falls
California

Staubbach
Switzerland

Tugela
South Africa

Sutherland
New Zealand

MAKING A PICTOGRAPH

Use an encyclopedia to find the five longest rivers in the world. Make a pictograph that compares the lengths of these rivers. Use drawings of rivers in your pictograph.

UNIT FOUR

Learning About the Human Body

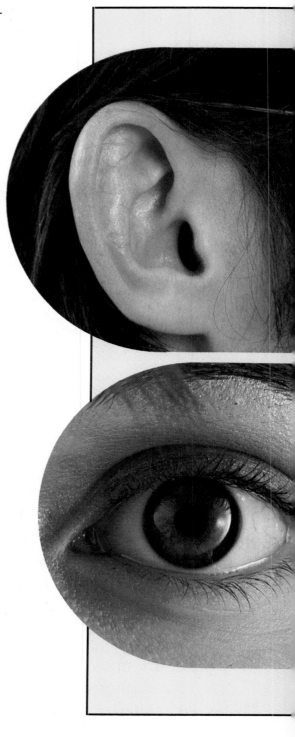

Think of what a perfect machine might be like if it could be built. A perfect machine might have a computer telling it how to move. It might have parts that would make the machine aware of its surroundings. And when it needed energy, a perfect machine might be able to supply itself with fuel.

In many ways, the human body is better than a perfect machine. The human body is made of millions of parts. It is controlled by a brain. Its eyes, ears, nose, tongue, and skin help to keep the body aware of its surroundings. The body is also able to take in food and use it for energy. In this unit you will learn more about a perfect machine—the human body.

266

Chapter 13

Using Food

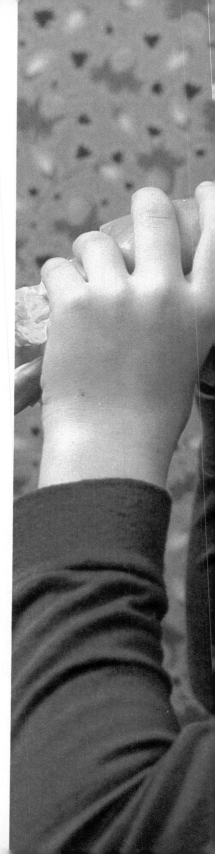

Why do you eat? You might think you eat because you feel hungry. What makes you feel hungry? Sometimes you feel hungry when you see, smell, or even think of food. But often you feel hungry because your body needs energy. Your body gets energy from the food you eat. So the main reason you eat is to supply your body with energy.

The body is able to break down large pieces of food into smaller pieces. It can then break down these smaller pieces into particles it can use for energy. In this chapter you will learn about the parts of the body that work together to do this job.

—FROM CELLS TO SYSTEMS—
What are cells, tissues, organs, and systems?

What are the smallest parts of your body? Are your hands the smallest parts? Are your fingers? How about your knuckles? No, none of these parts are the smallest. The smallest parts of your body are called **cells.** The body is made of millions of cells. Most of these cells are so small that you need a microscope to see them. Even the largest cell in the body is only about the size of a pinpoint. Look at the cells shown in the pictures on these pages. In these pictures the cells are hundreds of times larger than they are in the body.

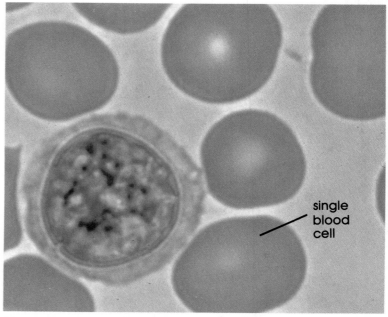

single blood cell

Blood cells

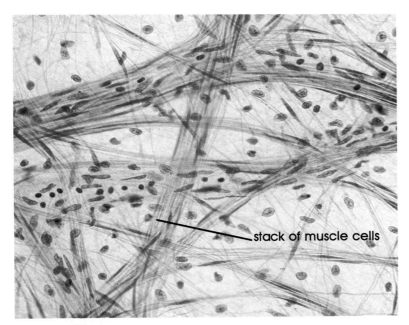
stack of muscle cells

Muscle cells

The body is made of different types of cells. Blood is made of blood cells, while muscles are made of muscle cells. As you can see in the pictures, different types of cells have different shapes and sizes. Blood cells are round, while muscle cells are long and thin.

Groups of cells work together to do certain jobs in the body. These groups of cells are called **tissues** (tish′üz). Muscle tissue is made of muscle cells. These cells work together to help move parts of the body. Bone tissue is made of bone cells. These cells work together to support parts of the body. What types of cells make up skin tissue? What do these cells work together to do?

Just as groups of cells work together to form tissues, groups of tissues also work together in the body. These groups of tissues form **organs** (ôr′gəns). Organs have special jobs in the body. Your heart is an organ that is made mainly of muscle tissue. The heart pumps blood throughout the body. Your brain is an organ that is made mainly of nervous tissue. The brain controls most of the body. What are some other organs in your body?

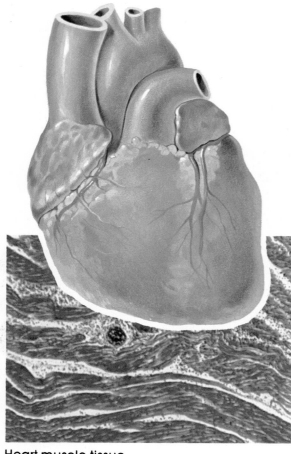

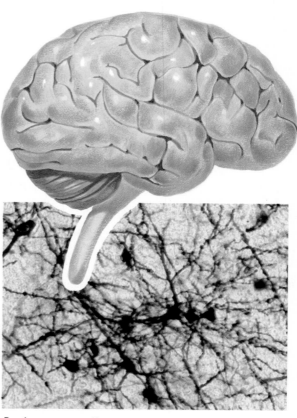

Heart muscle tissue

Brain nervous tissue

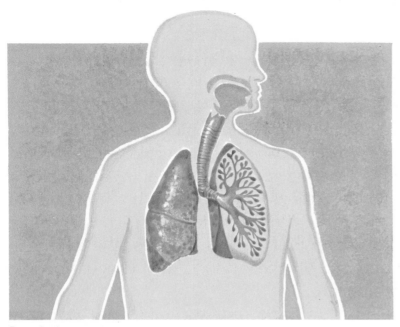
Respiratory system

So far, you have learned that your body is made of cells, tissues, and organs. Did you know that groups of cells, tissues, and organs also work together? These groups make up **systems** (sis′təms).

Your body has many important systems. The respiratory (res′pər ə tôr ē) system brings oxygen into the body and releases carbon dioxide from the body. Two parts of this system are the lungs and the windpipe. They are made of many types of tissues and cells.

Another important body system is the digestive (də jes′tiv) system. This system breaks down food so that it can be used by the body. You will learn more about this important body system in the rest of this chapter.

USING WHAT YOU EAT
What is digestion?

You eat many different types of food every day. You may have eggs or cereal for breakfast. Maybe you eat soup and a sandwich for lunch. After school you might eat a piece of fruit. You may eat chicken or fish with vegetables for dinner. Your body is able to take in and use all these foods. But why is food so important?

Food is important to your body in many ways. Food provides the materials the body needs to grow. Food is used by the body to repair and replace worn-out and damaged parts. Food also provides the energy needed by the cells. Without this energy, the parts of the body could not do their jobs.

Pieces of food that you eat are not in a form that can be used by your cells. Every piece of food you eat is much larger than any cell in your body. Also, a single piece of food may contain materials that are needed by different groups of cells in your body. So food must be changed into a form your cells can use. Changing food into a form your cells can use is called digestion. The system used to digest food is the **digestive system.**

To help you understand digestion, look at the picture. Food is first broken into small pieces in the mouth. These small pieces then travel down a tube into the stomach. There they are broken into tiny chemical particles. The chemical particles travel to the intestines (in tes'təns), where they enter the bloodstream.

food broken into small pieces in mouth

food traveling down tube into stomach

food broken into tiny chemical particles

food entering bloodstream

How is food digested in the mouth?

Your teeth are important to the way you look. They are also a very important part of your digestive system. Teeth help to carry out the first step of digestion.

Did you know that you have different kinds of teeth? The teeth in the front of your mouth are called **incisors** (in sī′zərs). Incisors are thin and flat. They have sharp edges that help to cut and bite food. Next to the incisors are pointed teeth called **canines** (kā′nīns). The sharp points of these teeth help to bite and tear food.

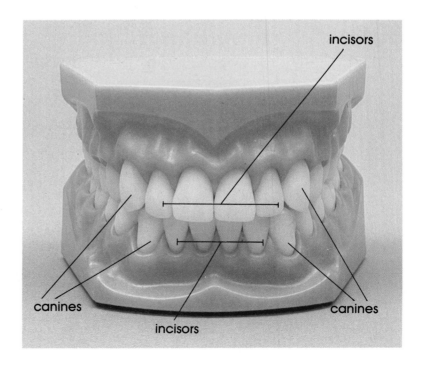

Next to the canine teeth are teeth with flat tops. These teeth are called **premolars** (prē mō′lərs). Premolars help to crush food into smaller pieces. The teeth at the back of your mouth are **molars** (mō′lərs). Molars have large flat tops that help to crush and grind food into smaller pieces. Look at these pictures. Then look in a mirror. Try to identify your teeth.

Digestion begins as soon as food enters your mouth. You bite and tear pieces of food with your incisors and canines. You grind food into smaller pieces with your premolars and molars. The longer you chew a piece of food, the smaller the pieces become.

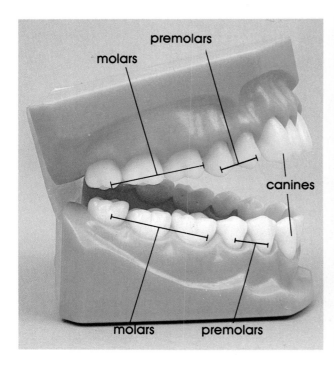

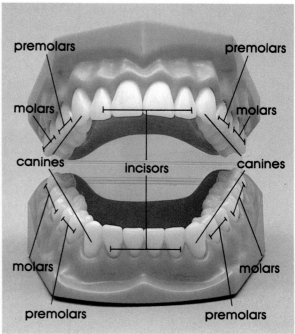

As you can see in the drawings, digestion in the mouth involves more than teeth. As you chew food, a juice called saliva (sə lī′və) is released. **Saliva** helps to make food wet and soft. Soft, wet food is easy to swallow. Saliva also helps to break down chemicals in food.

The whole time you are chewing your food, your **tongue** is moving the food around in your mouth. Your tongue helps to mix the food with saliva. When you swallow, your tongue pushes the food into the back of your mouth.

By the time you swallow, one step of digestion is complete. Your teeth, tongue, and saliva have made large pieces of food smaller, softer, and wetter. They have made it easier for the food to travel through the rest of the digestive system.

biting food

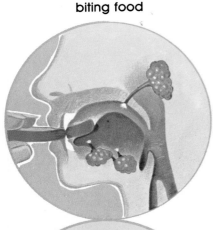

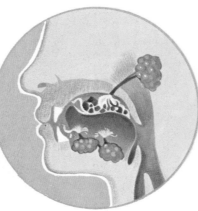

saliva

tongue

chewing food

release of saliva

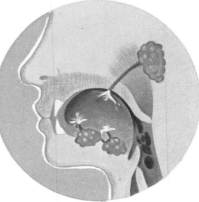

tongue mixing food
with saliva

tongue pushing food
to back of mouth

food swallowed

278

What happens to food in your mouth?

Materials   cracker / slice of bread / clock

Procedure

A. Take a few bites of a cracker. While looking at a clock, chew the cracker for 1 minute before you swallow it. Notice how the taste of the cracker changes as it mixes with saliva while you chew it.

1. What did the cracker taste like when you started chewing it?
2. How did the cracker taste after 1 minute?
3. Besides changing the taste, how else did saliva change the cracker as you chewed it?

B. Take a few bites of a slice of bread. Chew the bread for 1 minute.

4. What did the bread taste like when you started chewing it?
5. How did the bread taste after 1 minute?
6. Besides changing the taste, how else did saliva change the bread as you chewed it?

Conclusion

1. What happens to the taste of foods such as crackers and bread when they are mixed with saliva in the mouth?
2. What else happens to food in the mouth?

Using science ideas

Repeat step **A** using other foods, such as fruits, meats, and vegetables.

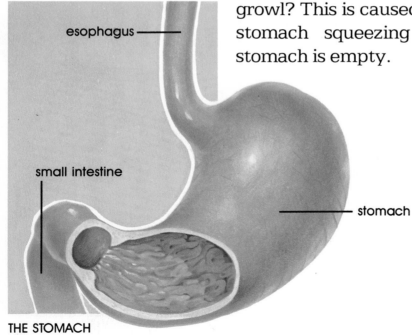

THE ESOPHAGUS

THE STOMACH

THE DIGESTIVE PATH

What happens to food after it is swallowed?

After food is swallowed, it enters a long hollow tube called the **esophagus** (ē sof′ə-gəs). The esophagus is made of strong muscles that push the food into the stomach. These muscles can push food even if you are standing on your head.

The **stomach** is a hollow organ that is shaped like the letter *J.* It is made mainly of muscles. Food in the stomach is mixed with juices. The juices come from cells in the wall of the stomach. They help to further digest the food. The muscles of the stomach squeeze together and mix the food and juices. Have you ever heard your stomach growl? This is caused by the muscles in your stomach squeezing together when your stomach is empty.

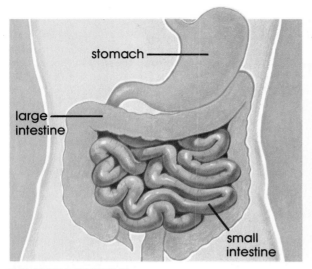

stomach

large intestine

small intestine

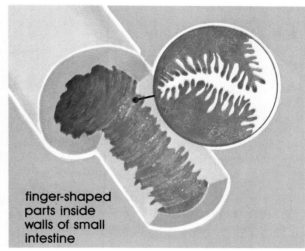

finger-shaped parts inside walls of small intestine

THE SMALL INTESTINE

When food leaves the stomach, it is a thick liquid. The thick liquid moves into the small intestine. The **small intestine** is an organ that is shaped like a long tube. It is about four times longer than your height. Muscles in the walls of the small intestine squeeze the food. The squeezing breaks the food into even smaller pieces. More juices are mixed with the food. Some of these juices come from the small intestine itself. Other juices come from organs connected to the small intestine.

As you can see in the drawing, the inside of the small intestine has parts that look like fingers. These finger-shaped parts contain many small tubes filled with blood. Tiny particles of food leave the small intestine and enter the bloodstream here. The blood carries the food to cells throughout the body.

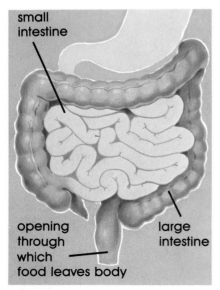

small intestine

opening through which food leaves body

large intestine

THE LARGE INTESTINE

Most of the food that the body uses enters the bloodstream through the small intestine. Food that does not enter the bloodstream moves into the large intestine. The **large intestine** is an organ that is shaped like a short wide tube. Water is removed from the food in this organ. Like the small intestine, the large intestine has finger-shaped parts. Water taken out of the food enters the bloodstream through these parts. Unused food leaves the body through an opening at the end of the large intestine. This completes digestion. Look at the table on page 283. It shows the steps in digestion.

THE DIGESTIVE SYSTEM		
	Body part	Part in digestion
	Mouth	• Teeth bite, chew, grind food • Saliva softens and wets food, breaks down some chemicals
	Esophagus	• Connects mouth with stomach
	Stomach	• Mixes food with juices that help break down food
	Small intestine	• Squeezes food • Mixes food with juices • Removes useful parts of food and releases them into bloodstream
	Large intestine	• Removes water from food and releases it into bloodstream

Finding out

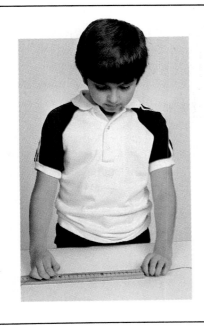

How long is a digestive path?   To get an idea of how long a digestive path is, you need a ball of string, a meterstick, and a pair of scissors. Measure 8 cm of string. This is about how deep your mouth is. Your esophagus is about 43 cm long. Measure another 43 cm of string. Your stomach is about 20 cm long. Measure another 20 cm of string. Your small intestine is much longer. It is about 6.4 m long. Measure another 6.4 m of string. Your large intestine is about 1.5 m long. Measure another 1.5 m of string. Cut the string at this point. Now measure the whole piece of string. How long is this digestive path?

What foods contain starch?

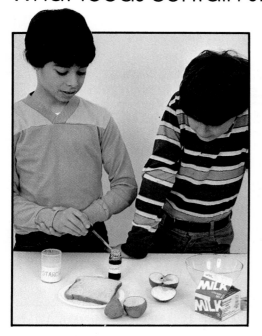

Materials   iodine solution / starch solution / medicine dropper / bread / other pieces of food

Procedure

A. One of the many chemicals your digestive system breaks down is starch. You can test a piece of food to see if it contains starch by using iodine. Get a container of iodine solution and another container of starch solution from your teacher. **Caution:** *Do not taste anything used in this activity.*

   1. What color is the iodine solution?
   2. What color is the starch solution?

B. With a medicine dropper, put a few drops of the iodine solution into the starch solution.

   3. What color does the starch solution become?

C. Put a few drops of the iodine solution on a piece of bread. If the bread becomes the same color as the starch did, then the bread contains starch.

   4. What color did the bread become?
   5. Does the bread contain starch?

D. Make a chart with headings like the one shown. Test other foods supplied by your teacher for starch. Complete the chart.

Conclusion

1. What color does starch become if iodine is added to it?
2. Which of the foods you tested contained starch?

Food	Color food turns when iodine is added	Does food contain starch?

— DIGESTIVE SYSTEM PROBLEMS —
How can you take care of your digestive system?

Has anyone ever told you that you should not exercise right after you eat? Do you know why? The muscles in your digestive system use energy. If you exercise while these muscles are working, you take away some of the energy they need. This can cause stomach cramps. Stomach cramps can be painful. You could drown if you get them while you are swimming. Because of this, you should not do any active exercise right after you eat.

Like most people, you have probably had a stomachache. Stomachaches are a common problem of the digestive system. A stomachache can be very painful. It can be caused by eating too much food. It can also be caused by eating food that is very spicy. Stomachaches usually go away after a short time. They can be prevented by taking care of the digestive system.

One way you can take care of your digestive system is to eat the proper kinds of foods. You should not eat too many fatty or fried foods. You should not eat too many foods that are very spicy. What you should eat are plenty of fruits and vegetables. These foods contain a material called fiber. Many doctors think that foods with fiber help to keep the digestive system healthy.

Fruits and vegetables

IDEAS TO REMEMBER

▶ Your body is made up of cells, tissues, organs, and systems.

▶ The digestive system changes food into a form the cells in the body can use.

▶ Food travels from the mouth to the stomach through the esophagus. From the stomach, food travels to the small intestine, and then to the large intestine.

▶ Stomachaches and stomach cramps are common digestive system problems.

▶ One way you can take care of your digestive system is to eat the proper kinds of foods.

Reviewing the Chapter

SCIENCE WORDS

A. Use all the terms below to complete the sentences.

saliva   incisors   stomach   molars
canines   esophagus   tongue   premolars
large intestine   small intestine

     The digestion of food begins in the mouth. Teeth called __1__ and __2__ bite and tear food. The __3__ and __4__ grind the food. At the same time a juice called __5__ helps make the food wet and soft. Before swallowing, the __6__ pushes the food into the back of the mouth. After the food is swallowed, it first enters a long tube called the __7__. The food then moves first into the __8__, and then into the __9__, and finally into the __10__.

B. Identify each of the following.

1. I am a group of cells, tissues, and organs. What am I?
2. I am the smallest parts of the body. What am I?
3. I am a group of tissues that work together. What am I?
4. I am a body system that changes food into a form that the cells can use. What am I?
5. I am a group of cells. What am I?

UNDERSTANDING IDEAS

A. Tell which of the following sentences are true and which are false.

1. Muscle cells work together to help move parts of the body.
2. The cells that make up skin are the same as the cells that make up bones.
3. Groups of cells work together to do certain jobs.
4. Bone tissue is made of blood cells.
5. The brain is made mainly of nervous tissue.

B. Identify each of these parts of the digestive system. Explain how each part helps in digestion.

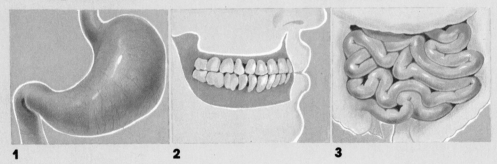

1   2   3

C. Explain what problems you might have with your digestive system. Describe the proper care for your digestive system.

USING IDEAS

1. You may have heard the saying "You are what you eat." Use reference books to find out what foods are good for you. Plan a 3-day menu that contains these foods.

Chapter 14

The Sense Organs

What was the first thing you noticed when you woke up this morning? Was it bright sunlight? The smell of breakfast? The cold air in your room? The sound of an alarm clock? Your senses might have let you know about many things at once.

Your senses link your body to the world around you. You see with your eyes and hear with your ears. Your nose and mouth help you smell and taste. The skin covering your body helps you touch objects and feel pain, cold, and heat.

In this chapter you will learn about the senses and the sense organs. You will find out how your senses help you enjoy the world and keep you safe in it.

– SENSE ORGANS AND THE BRAIN –

How do sense organs and the brain work together?

Can you name the five senses? The five senses are seeing, hearing, tasting, smelling, and touching. Each of these senses depends on special organs in the body. These organs are called **sense organs.** The eyes, ears, tongue, nose, and skin are the sense organs. What sense organs are the people in these pictures using?

Your sense organs do not work alone. You do not see with just your eyes or hear with just your ears. Your sense organs are connected to your brain. How do the sense organs send information to your brain?

The brain is made of billions of nerve cells closely packed together. Other nerve cells lead from the brain to all parts of the body. These nerve cells join together to form nerves. The nerves send signals to and from the brain. The endings of some nerves are in your sense organs.

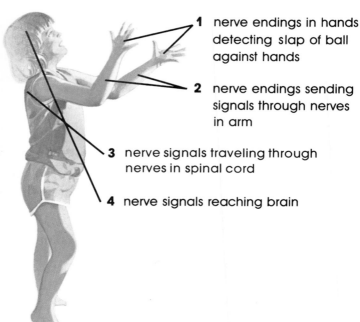

1 nerve endings in hands detecting slap of ball against hands

2 nerve endings sending signals through nerves in arm

3 nerve signals traveling through nerves in spinal cord

4 nerve signals reaching brain

In the drawing you can see how nerve signals are sent when the girl catches the ball. Trace this path with your finger as you read. First, nerve endings in the hands detect the slap of the ball against the hands. The nerve endings send signals through the nerves in the arm to nerves in the spinal cord. The signals travel through the spinal cord to the brain. When they reach the brain, the girl is aware of catching the ball.

Signals can move very quickly along nerves. Some signals can travel over 90 m in 1 second. Why would it be so important for these signals to travel quickly if you touched a hot stove?

THE EYE AND SIGHT

How does the eye work?

Did you ever stop to think how useful the sense of sight is? With the sense of sight, you can see things that are tiny, like an insect on a flower. You can also see large objects, such as trees and buildings. You can read this page when it is close to you. You can also see stars that are billions of kilometers away. You can notice the color of a sunset or the movement of a cat in tall grass. How are you able to see so many different things?

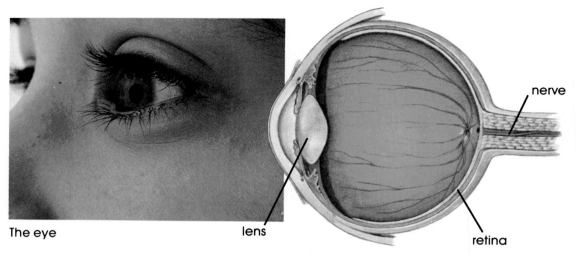

The eye

nerve

lens

retina

The eye contains special cells that can detect light. When light hits an object, some of the light bounces off the object. You see the object because some of this light enters your eyes.

As you can see in the drawing, light entering the eye goes through a lens. The **lens** is a clear part of the eye. It is made of living cells. The lens bends light. The bent light forms a tiny picture on the back wall of the eye.

The back wall of the eye is called the **retina** (ret′ə nə). The retina has millions of cells in it. These cells are close to nerve endings. When light from an object hits the cells, the nerve endings pick up signals. These signals are passed along a nerve that leads to the brain. The brain then "tells" parts of the body how to react toward what the eye saw. How would your body react to a juicy hamburger?

The lenses in the eyes of some people do not bend light correctly. Clear pictures do not always form on the retinas of their eyes. Sometimes a person can clearly see only things that are near. Such a person is said to be nearsighted. A farsighted person can clearly see only things that are far away. Some people who are nearsighted or farsighted wear eyeglasses. Eyeglasses are made of glass or plastic. They help the eye to bend light correctly. This helps the person to see things clearly.

Finding out

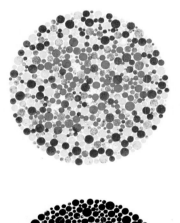

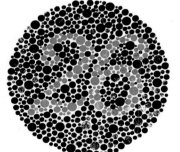

How can you tell if you are color-blind? The retina of the eye is made up of different types of cells. Some of these cells can detect colors. Sometimes people are born without certain kinds of these cells. These people are said to be color-blind. Some color-blind people cannot see green colors. Others cannot see red colors.

You can find out if you are color-blind by looking at these drawings. If you see a 29 in the top circle and a 26 in the bottom circle, you are not color-blind. If you see only a 6 in the bottom circle, you are red-blind. If you see only a 2 in the bottom circle, you are green-blind. If you see a 70 in the top circle and nothing in the other circle, you are red-and green-blind. If you cannot see any numbers in either circle, you are totally color-blind. If you are not color-blind, maybe someone in your family is. Give this test to other members of your family.

Eye protection

Eye protection

Having eyes checked by a doctor

People often take their eyes for granted. But it is easy to injure your eyes if you are not careful. Some household cleaners can sting or burn your eyes. While playing sports you can poke your eyes with balls, sticks, and rackets. Another way your eyes can be hurt is by looking right at the sun.

You can help to prevent lifelong damage by taking care of your eyes if anything happens to them. You should not rub your eyes if dirt gets in them. Tears usually wash dirt out of your eyes. Specks of dirt that do not wash out should be removed by a doctor. If any harmful liquid gets in them, you should rinse your eyes with warm water for several minutes. Above all, you should have your eyes checked regularly by a doctor. In this way you will be taking good care of one of your most important senses.

THE EARS AND HEARING

How does the ear work?

Have you ever known about something happening far away without seeing it happen? Maybe you first knew about a parade by the sounds of music. You might have known a frog was nearby when you heard its croak. Hearing is another important sense that tells you about the world.

You can hear when sound waves reach the ear. Sound waves cause particles of air to vibrate, or move back and forth. The ear picks up sound waves.

As you can see in the drawing, the part of the body that most people call the ear is just the **outer ear.** The outer ear catches sound waves and guides them into the **ear canal.** The vibrating air in the ear canal causes the eardrum to vibrate. The **eardrum** is a thin tissue at the end of the ear canal. The eardrum is close to three small bones that make up the **middle ear.** When the eardrum vibrates, so do the three bones. They pass the vibrations to the **inner ear.**

In the inner ear is a long coiled tube that looks like a snail's shell. The tube is filled with a liquid. When the liquid vibrates, it moves the tiny hairlike nerve endings that are found in the tube. The nerve endings send signals to the brain.

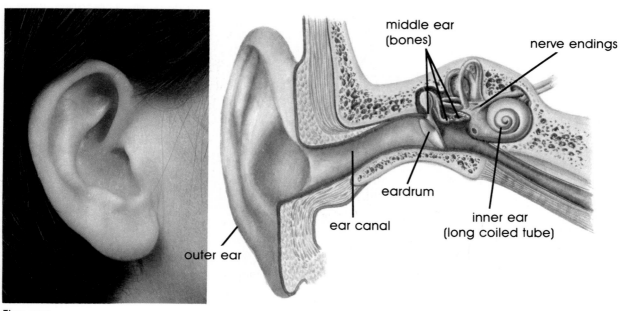

The ear

Some sounds can be harmful to a person's ears. Sudden loud noises can tear the eardrum or damage the nerve endings of the inner ear. They can cause loss of hearing. Constant noise can also be harmful. Factory workers often spend many hours around loud machines. The noise can make them lose some of their hearing.

You can help take care of your ears by staying away from noisy places. If you must be in a noisy place, you should protect your ears the way the person in the picture is. Also, you should never stick anything in your ears. Your doctor can show you the correct way to clean your ears. Your doctor can also check your ears to make sure you are hearing properly.

Ear protection

— THE TONGUE AND THE NOSE —

How are you able to taste and smell?

Remember the last time you had a bad cold? Your food probably didn't seem to have much flavor. Most people think they use only their tongue to taste food. But the odors your nose picks up also help to give food its flavor. This is why it is difficult for a person with a stuffy nose to taste food.

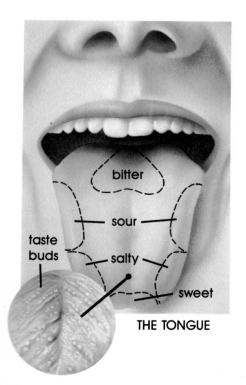

THE TONGUE

Have you ever taken a close look at your tongue? It is covered with tiny bumps. Each bump has several **taste buds** in it. Each taste bud is made up of cells that are connected to nerve endings. The taste of food is picked up by these nerve cells.

The tongue can only detect four different tastes. It can tell whether something is sweet, sour, salty, or bitter. As you can see in the drawing, taste buds in different areas of the tongue detect different tastes. On what part of your tongue could you taste a piece of cake?

Where are different flavors tasted on the tongue?

Materials   4 clean cotton swabs / 4 paper cups containing liquids

Procedure
A. Your teacher will provide four paper cups, each filled with a liquid. Dip a clean cotton swab into the paper cup labeled *A*.

B. Touch the cotton swab to the tip of a classmate's tongue. Then touch the back and the sides of the tongue.
   1. How did your classmate think liquid *A* tasted—sweet, sour, salty, or bitter?
   2. On what part of the tongue did your classmate taste the liquid?

C. Draw a picture of a tongue. Label where liquid *A* was tasted. Label whether liquid *A* was sweet, sour, salty, or bitter.

D. Repeat steps **A, B,** and **C** with the other cups of liquid.
   3. How did your classmate think each liquid tasted?
   4. On what part of the tongue did your classmate taste each liquid?

Conclusion
1. On what parts of the tongue did your classmate taste the sweet liquid? The sour liquid? The salty liquid? The bitter liquid?
2. Are any flavors tasted on more than one part of the tongue?

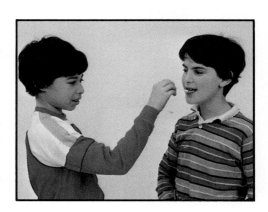

303

In the back of the inside of the nose are thousands of nerve endings. You can see where they are in the drawing. When you breathe normally, very little air goes into this part of the nose. But what happens when you sniff air? Sniffing causes air to rush up into the back of the nose. There the nerve endings pick up odors in the air. The nerve endings send signals to the brain. Have you ever sniffed a flower? Signals your brain gets from sniffing a flower let you know how good the flower smells.

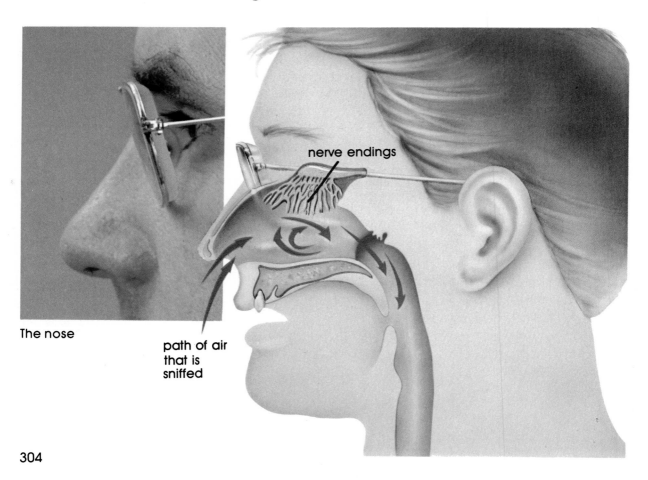

The nose

nerve endings

path of air that is sniffed

THE SKIN

What are some of the things your skin can detect?

Your fifth sense organ, the skin, can detect many different things. Some of these things are shown here. Your skin can detect a mosquito on your arm. It can tell warm from cold. If someone squeezes your hand, your skin can detect pressure. The skin also lets you feel pain. How can the skin do all these things?

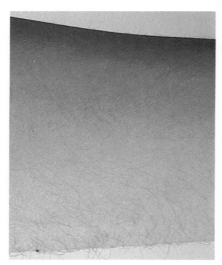
The skin

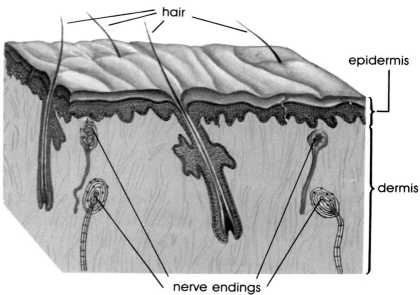

Look at the drawing. As you can see, the top layer of the skin is the **epidermis** (ep ə-dėr'mis). The epidermis has a thin water-proof covering made of dead cells. Below the epidermis is a thicker layer, called the **dermis** (dėr'mis).

There are many different types of nerve endings in the skin. Some of the nerve endings are used when you touch something. Other nerve endings detect pain, pressure, and changes in temperature. You might not think that having a sense organ that detects pain is important. But the skin is very important. Feeling pain is the way your body warns you that something is wrong. Can you imagine not being able to know that you cut your foot? What could happen if you could not feel this kind of pain?

Besides being a sense organ, the skin also protects you. It keeps out germs and helps to keep your body warm. It also protects you from the sun.

To care for your skin, you should keep it clean. You should also properly treat cuts. A cut should be washed and covered with a bandage. Taking care of your skin is one way you can stay healthy.

Caring for the skin

Do you know?

Most people don't think about how important their sense of touch is. But to people who are blind, the sense of touch allows them to read.

A blind person can read by using the Braille (brāl) system. The Braille system consists of small raised dots on a piece of paper. The Braille alphabet consists of 63 different groups of dots. By moving their fingers across these groups of dots, blind people can read them. This is an example of someone using one sense to make up for the loss of another sense.

What can you identify with your sense of touch?

Materials   box with holes in it containing un-known objects

Procedure

A. Without looking inside, put your hands into the box your teacher gives you.

B. Use your sense of touch to examine one of the objects in the box.
   1. About how big is the object?
   2. What shape is it?
   3. How does the surface of the object feel?
   4. What other properties can you describe?
   5. What do you think the object is?

C. Without looking at the other objects, re-move this object from the box.
   6. What is it?
   7. Did you correctly identify the object be-fore you saw it? If not, what properties caused you to be wrong?

D. Repeat steps **A, B,** and **C** with the other ob-jects in the box.

Conclusion

1. How many of the objects in the box did you correctly identify?
2. Which properties were the most helpful in correctly identifying the objects?
3. Which properties were you unable to detect with your sense of touch?

IDEAS TO REMEMBER

▶ The eyes, ears, tongue, nose, and skin are the sense organs. Each of the sense organs is connected to the brain by nerves.

▶ Light that bounces off objects enters the eye and passes through the lens. A picture of the object forms on the back wall of the eye, called the retina.

▶ Sound waves enter the outer ear and pass into the ear canal. They cause the eardrum to vibrate, which causes the bones of the middle ear to vibrate. These bones pass the vibrations on to the inner ear.

▶ Both the nose and the tongue are used to taste foods.

▶ The skin can detect pain, pressure, and changes in temperature.

Reviewing the Chapter

SCIENCE WORDS

A. Write the letter of the term that best matches the definition. Not all the terms will be used.

1. The tiny bumps on the tongue that are made up of cells connected to nerve endings
2. The top layer of skin
3. The back wall of the eye
4. The eyes, ears, tongue, nose, and skin
5. The part of the eye that bends light

  a. taste buds
  b. lens
  c. retina
  d. outer ear
  e. dermis
  f. sense organs
  g. epidermis

B. Use all the terms below to complete the sentences.

eardrum   outer ear   inner ear
ear canal   middle ear

In order to hear, the __1__ must catch sound waves. The sound waves are guided into the __2__, and at its end they reach a thin tissue. This tissue is called the __3__. As this tissue vibrates, it causes the three bones that make up the __4__ to vibrate, too. These bones pass the vibrations along to the __5__.

UNDERSTANDING IDEAS

A. Explain how the sense organs send information to the brain.

B. Identify each of the following sense organs. Write the correct term for each number in the diagram. Tell how the sense organs work.

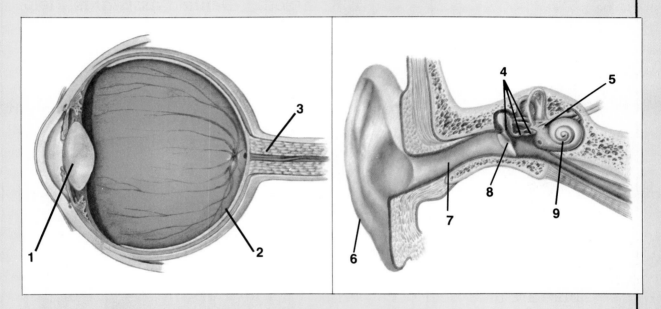

C. Explain how to care for your eyes and ears.

USING IDEAS

1. Pretend you are a scientist who has made a robot. Write a report explaining how you made the robot's sense organs. Discuss some of the experiences your robot has had.

2. Use reference books to find out what people who are blind can do to overcome their loss of sight.

Science in Careers

Another group of careers in the health field involves medicine. There are many careers in medicine. *Dentists* treat people who have problems with their teeth. *Dental assistants* help the dentists. *Nurses* and *doctors* care for people who are sick or hurt. *Medical laboratory workers* do tests for doctors. These tests help the doctor find out what is wrong with someone.

Medical laboratory worker

There are a number of careers for people interested in helping other people stay healthy. One group of these careers involves food. *Dietitians* are people who plan meals for other people. Many dietitians work in hospitals and schools. *Chefs* are people who prepare food. The food prepared by a chef must be tasty and must look good.

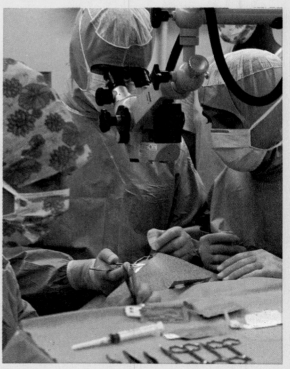

Doctor and nurse

People in Science

Adelle Davis (1904–1974)

Adelle Davis was born and raised on a farm in central Indiana. As a youngster she was active in the 4-H Club. Davis went to college at Purdue University, where she studied nutrition. Nutrition is the study of how food is used by the body. For most of her life, Davis tried to educate Americans about nutrition. She felt that Americans ate too many foods containing salt and sugar. Davis also felt that a proper diet should include fresh fruits and vegetables.

Foods that are part of a proper diet

313

Developing Skills

WORD SKILLS

Many English words have word parts that come from other languages. This table lists word parts that come from other languages and gives their meanings. Use the table to help you write a definition for each of the words listed.

1. auditory
2. carbohydrate
3. endoderm
4. monocle
5. stereoscopic
6. stereophonic

Word part	Meaning
audio-	hearing
carbo-	relating to carbon
endo-	inner
hydro-	water
mono-	one
phon-	sound
stereo-	three-dimensional
-ar	resembling
-ate	having to do with
-derm	skin
-ic	one that produces
-ocul, -ocle	eye
-scope	for seeing
-tory	relating to

READING A BAR GRAPH

Look at the bar graph on the next page. A bar graph can be used to compare information. This bar graph compares the number of Calories used up each hour that certain activities are performed. Use the bar graph to answer the following questions.

1. Which of the activities shown uses up the most Calories in 1 hour?

2. Which of the activities shown uses up the least Calories in 1 hour?

3. Which activity uses up more Calories in 1 hour, jogging or jumping rope?

4. Which activity uses up more Calories in 1 hour, walking or jogging?

5. How many more Calories are used up in playing baseball for 1 hour than in walking for 1 hour?

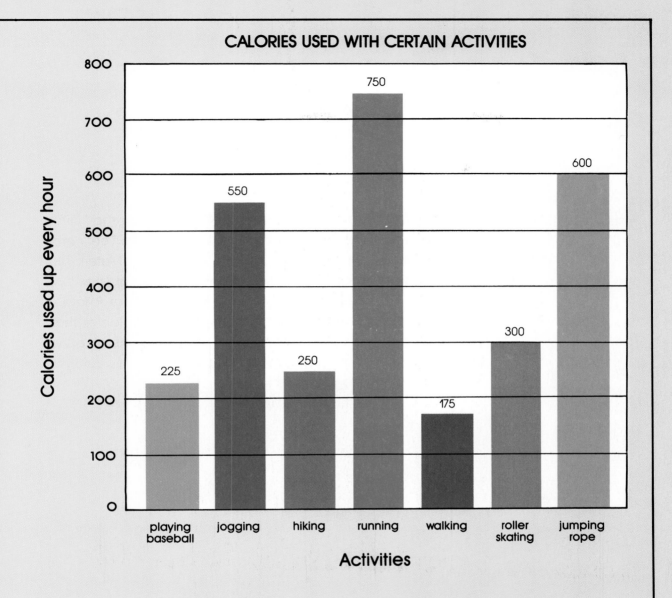

CALORIES USED WITH CERTAIN ACTIVITIES

Calories used up every hour

Activity	Calories
playing baseball	225
jogging	550
hiking	250
running	750
walking	175
roller skating	300
jumping rope	600

Activities

MAKING A BAR GRAPH

Find a reference book that lists Calories contained in various foods. Make a bar graph that compares the number of Calories in the same amount of water, a fruit juice, whole milk, and a soft drink.

Units of Measurement

Two systems of measurement are used in the United States, the metric system and the English system. Feet, yards, pounds, ounces, and quarts are English units. Meters, kilometers, kilograms, grams, and liters are metric units. Only metric measurements are used in science. The following tables list some metric and English units. The tables show what each unit is approximately equal to in the other system. The metric mass/English weight relationships hold true for objects on the earth.

MEASUREMENT	METRIC UNITS (symbol)	EQUAL TO IN ENGLISH UNITS (symbol)
Length	1 millimeter (mm)	0.04 inch (in.)
	1 centimeter (cm)	0.4 inch (in.)
	1 meter (m)	39.4 inches (in.) or
		1.1 yards (yd)
	1 kilometer (km)	0.6 mile (mi)
Mass (weight)	1 gram (g)	0.035 ounce (oz)
	1 kilogram (kg)	2.2 pounds (lb)
Volume	1 liter (L)	1.06 quarts (qt)

MEASUREMENT	ENGLISH UNITS (symbol)	EQUAL TO IN METRIC UNITS (symbol)
Length	1 inch (in.)	2.5 centimeters (cm) or
		25 millimeters (mm)
	1 foot (ft)	30.5 centimeters (cm)
	1 yard (yd)	0.91 meter (m)
	1 mile (mi)	1.6 kilometers (km)
Weight (mass)	1 ounce (oz)	28.4 grams (g)
	1 pound (lb)	0.45 kilogram (kg)
Volume	1 quart (qt)	0.95 liter (L)

Lesson Questions

To the student

Reading your book will help you learn more about the world around you. Your book will provide answers to many questions you may have about living things, the earth, space, matter, and energy.

On the following pages you will find questions from each lesson in your book. These questions will help test your understanding of the terms and ideas you read about.

There are two kinds of questions. You can answer the first kind by using the information you read in each lesson. Careful reading will help answer these questions.

The second type of question is called "Thinking like a Scientist." These questions are more challenging. The answer may not be found just by reading the lesson. You may have to think harder.

1 Animals That Live Together

AN ANIMAL TOWN
(pp. 4–8)

1. What is an animal population?
2. What are these prairie dogs doing? Why are they doing it?

Thinking like a Scientist
Scientists draw conclusions about animals based on their sizes and shapes. Name several animals that burrow underground. What body shape do these animals have? How is this shape helpful? What problems would a giraffe or a hippopotamus have as a burrowing animal? What conclusions could a scientist draw about burrowing animals?

INSECT COLONIES
(pp. 9–12)

1. Name three types of bees in a honeybee colony. Tell what each type of bee does.
2. How do bees help people?

Thinking like a Scientist
Tell which member of the bee colony you think is the most important. Why do you think it is more important than any of the others?

SCHOOLS OF FISH
(pp. 13–15)

1. What is a school?
2. Give two reasons that fish swim in schools.

Thinking like a Scientist
How might the schooling behavior of fish help people who fish for a living? How might schooling become a problem?

ANIMAL HERDS

(pp. 16–18)

1. Write the letter of each group of animals that would be called a herd.

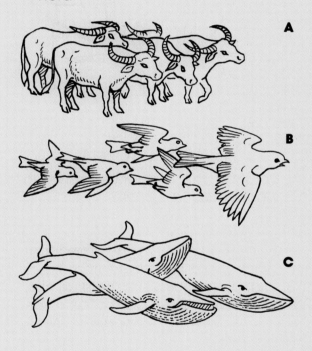

A

B

C

2. When do caribou herds form?

Thinking like a Scientist

Not long ago, large herds of buffalo roamed the plains of America. Hunting has made the buffalo an endangered animal. How did living in herds contribute to the decrease in the buffalo population? If the same-sized herds were returned to the plains today, what new problems would they have?

OTHER ANIMALS THAT LIVE TOGETHER

(pp. 19–21)

1. What is a parasite?
2. How does a flea harm a dog?
3. How do a clownfish and a sea anemone help each other?

Thinking like a Scientist

A certain kind of mosquito carries a disease called yellow fever. Tell why this can be a problem for human beings.

2 The World of Plants

GROUPING PLANTS
(pp. 26–28)

1. Why is it important to classify living things?
2. What are the two major groups to which all plants belong?

Thinking like a Scientist

Suppose that a space probe sends back reports of plants on a planet in another solar system. What would be the three most important pieces of information you would like to have about the plants? Write three questions about the new plants.

FLOWERING SEED PLANTS
(pp. 29–32)

1. Identify the pistil, petals, ovary, stamen, and seeds by using the letters in this drawing.

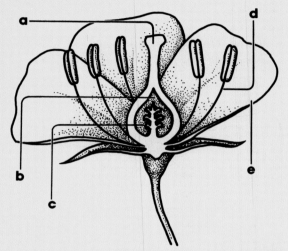

2. Describe the difference between monocots and dicots.

Thinking like a Scientist

In animals the most important body parts are protected from injury by special structures like the skull, ribs, and hipbone. Which parts of a flowering plant are most important? Why? How are these parts protected?

CONE-BEARING SEED PLANTS

(pp. 33–35)

1. Describe two differences between seed plants with flowers and seed plants with cones.
2. Identify each of the following conifers as either a pine, a hemlock, or a cedar.

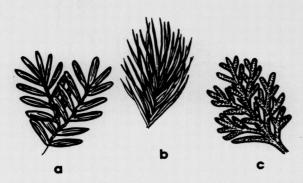

a   **b**   **c**

Thinking like a Scientist

Many plants produce seeds in flowers. In many of these plants the flowers change to a fruit. The seeds are found inside the fruit. The seeds of cones that produce trees are found inside the scales of the cones. What advantage do you think seeds produced in fruit have over seeds produced in cones?

NONSEED PLANTS

(pp. 36–43)

1. How are ferns different from mosses, fungi, and algae?
2. How are fungi different from all other plants?
3. What is one way to classify algae?

Thinking like a Scientist

Imagine that you are a scientist exploring a deep, damp cave for signs of plant life. List some plants that you might expect to find. Where do you think they might be growing?

3 Food Chains and Food Webs

LIVING THINGS NEED ENERGY
(pp. 48–49)

1. How are green plants different from other living things?
2. Explain how a producer is different from a consumer.

Thinking like a Scientist

Some animals, like seed-eating birds, eat many times during the day. Other animals, like some snakes, may eat only once a week. How can you explain the difference in the eating habits of these animals?

ANIMALS AND THEIR FOOD
(pp. 50–53)

1. Is this animal a herbivore or a carnivore? Why?

2. Is this animal a herbivore or a carnivore? Why?

Thinking like a Scientist

Herbivores, carnivores, and omnivores differ in their eating habits. Which one has the best chance of survival? Explain your answer.

FOOD CHAINS
(pp. 54–57)

1. What is a food chain?
2. What does a food chain always begin with?

3. Name the one animal that does not belong in each food chain.
   a. grass   grasshopper
      butterfly   frog   fish
   b. seeds   mouse   snake
      rabbit   hawk
4. Copy the following items. Draw arrows to show a food chain.
   bass   mayfly nymphs   blue herons
   shiners   plants

Thinking like a Scientist

Look at the food chain on page 55. What would happen to the food chain if a disease killed all the deer mice?

FOOD WEBS
(pp. 58–60)

1. What do all the plants and animals in one area make up?
2. What does a food web show?

3. Use names and arrows to show how the living things in the food web below are connected.

Thinking like a Scientist

Weather conditions such as floods, droughts, and extreme hot or cold temperatures can affect animals in many ways. Sometimes the weather can affect a food web. Give an example of a problem that might be caused by the weather.

4 How Living Things Survive

WHY LIVING THINGS ARE DIFFERENT
(pp. 66–67)

1. What is an adaptation?
2. Give an example of a plant adaptation?
3. Give an example of an activity that is an animal adaptation.

Thinking like a Scientist
Ducks have webbed feet. Robins do not have webbed feet. Tell how these adaptations help each animal survive.

TREES CHANGE WITH THE SEASONS
(pp. 68–70)

1. Identify the adaptation in the drawings. How does the adaptation help the plant survive?

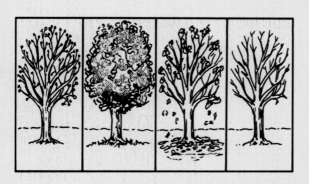

2. Explain how pine trees survive in cold climates without losing their leaves.

Thinking like a Scientist
The giant sequoia is a tree with needles. The needles spray a fine mist of water over the tree at certain times. How might this adaptation help the tree survive?

PLANT ADAPTATIONS
(pp. 71–74)

1. Name this plant adaptation. What is it used for?

2. Describe how a cactus plant's roots are a type of adaptation.

Thinking like a Scientist

Water lilies are plants that live in ponds. They have adaptations that allow their leaves to float on top of the water. How does this help water lilies survive?

ANIMAL ADAPTATIONS
(pp. 75–79)

1. Name two birds that feed on fish but have different beaks.
2. Explain why beaks help birds survive.

Thinking like a Scientist

A duck-billed platypus is not a bird. Yet it has a ducklike bill and webbed feet. Based on this description, tell where the platypus lives and what it eats.

WINTER ADAPTATIONS OF ANIMALS
(pp. 80–83)

1. Why do animals migrate?
2. What is another adaptation that helps animals survive winter?
3. Name an animal that uses this form of adaptation.

Thinking like a Scientist

Have you ever heard of Groundhog Day? On this day it is said that groundhogs crawl out of their burrow. If they see their shadow, there are supposed to be six more weeks of winter weather. What does Groundhog Day tell you about the adaptations of a groundhog? Do you believe that when a groundhog sees its shadow, six more weeks of winter will follow? Explain your answer.

5 *Measuring Matter*

THE PROPERTIES OF MATTER
(pp. 94–95)

1. Give the definition of matter.
2. What is a property?

Thinking like a Scientist

Choose an object in the classroom. Name the properties that cannot be measured.

THE LENGTH OF MATTER
(pp. 96–98)

1. In what units would it be best to measure each of the following distances?

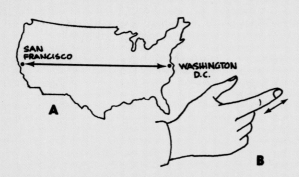

Thinking like a Scientist

Sometimes exact measurement of the length is not important. At these times we can estimate length. Describe two situations when measuring accurately would not be necessary.

MASS OF MATTER
(pp. 99–102)

1. Rewrite the following list so that the object with the least mass is first and the object with the greatest mass is last.
armchair   pencil   thumbtack
car   shoe   piano
2. Describe how you would measure a book, using a balance.

Thinking like a Scientist

Weight is a measure of gravitational pull. Mass is a measure of the amount of matter in an object. Compare measurements of mass and weight of an astronaut in outer space to mass and weight on earth.

VOLUME
(pp. 103–106)

1. Write the volume of each of the following:

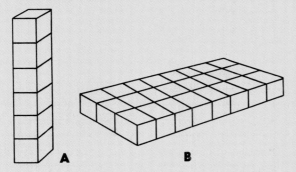

A   B

2. What tool would you use to measure the volume of a liquid?
3. Describe the three steps shown to find the volume of a marble.

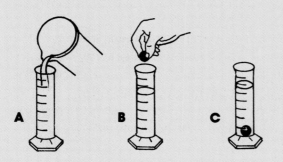

A   B   C

Thinking like a Scientist

Estimating volume can be a useful problem-solving skill. Describe an emergency or problem situation in which estimating volume would be helpful.

DENSITY
(pp. 107–109)

1. Rewrite the list of different kinds of matter below. Write them in order from the one with the least density to the one with the greatest density.

    water   iron   wood   air

2. What simple test would prove that a solid has greater density than a liquid?

Thinking like a Scientist

What inventions have helped people to measure matter? Identify at least ten inventions and what they measure.

6 Energy and Machines

FORMS OF ENERGY
(pp. 114–116)

1. What is energy?
2. What kind of energy does food contain?
3. What three kinds of energy are involved when a light bulb is turned on?

Thinking like a Scientist

Imagine that you are watching workers build a tall building. Describe six situations where energy is either stored or being used. Name the kind of energy in each situation.

TWO KINDS OF ENERGY
(pp. 117–119)

1. What is kinetic energy?
2. Imagine that you were trying to knock down a wall with a bowling ball. If you couldn't knock down the wall, what two changes could you make to knock it down?

3. What is stored energy called?
4. Look at this drawing of a roller-coaster track.

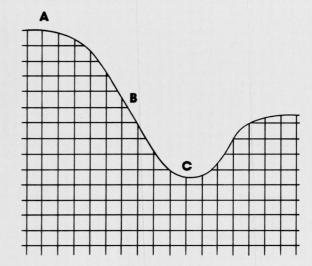

a. At what point will the roller-coaster car have the least potential energy?
b. At what point will it have the most potential energy?
c. At what point will it have the least kinetic energy?
d. At what point will it have the most kinetic energy?

Thinking like a Scientist

Describe a situation in which potential energy changes to electrical energy, then to kinetic energy, and back to potential energy.

SIMPLE MACHINES AND ENERGY
(pp. 120–125)

1. Identify the force, the fulcrum, and the load in the picture of the lever.

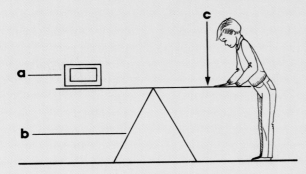

2. Does using a lever save energy? Explain your answer.

3. How is a force needed to use a fixed pulley different from the force needed to use a movable pulley?
4. What are two ways to reduce friction?

Thinking like a Scientist

How could each of these things be used to reduce friction: baby powder, a plastic bag, a pencil, marbles, and soap?

COMPOUND MACHINES AND ENERGY
(pp. 126–129)

1. What is a compound machine?
2. Name three wheel-and-axle machines in a bicycle.

Thinking like a Scientist

Name and describe the simple machines found in the following compound machines: hand drill, windup toy car, fishing rod and reel.

7 Heat Energy

HEAT
(pp. 134–135)

1. Describe the effect of heat energy on particles of matter.
2. How is heat measured?
3. What is a unit of heat energy called?

Thinking like a Scientist

How can we tell if matter contains heat energy without touching it? Suppose one cardboard box contained a very hot rock (120°C). Another box contains a cold rock of the same size and material. Both boxes have small holes in the lid. Name at least three ways to tell which box contains the hot rock without touching the boxes or placing a thermometer near them.

HEAT AND TEMPERATURE
(pp. 136–138)

1. What does temperature measure?
2. In what unit is temperature measured?

3. The water in both of these bowls is the same temperature. Which of these bowls of water contains more heat? Why?

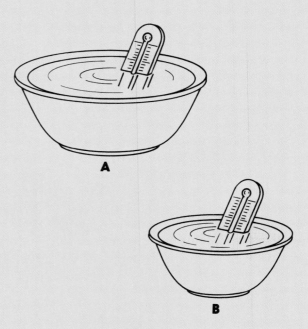

Thinking like a Scientist

Imagine a burning match and a large burning bonfire. Compare these two fires in terms of both their heat and temperature.

HOW HEAT MOVES THROUGH SOLID MATTER
(pp. 139–142)

1. Describe how heat moves from soup to the handle of a spoon sitting in the soup.
2. What makes some materials good insulators?

Thinking like a Scientist
Some people make pans for a living. What should they know about the movement of heat?

HOW HEAT MOVES THROUGH LIQUIDS AND GASES
(pp. 143–144)

1. What is the way that heat energy moves through liquids and gases called?
2. Describe how an entire room can be heated by one heater.

Thinking like a Scientist
Some people use ceiling fans in winter to keep their heated houses warmer. How do you suppose the fans help?

HEAT FROM SUNLIGHT
(pp. 145–147)

1. What is the movement of heat energy in waves called?
2. Describe how you can be warmed by the sun.
3. Why are greenhouses used for growing plants?

Thinking like a Scientist
Pets are often accidentally killed by heat in closed cars during hot weather. Explain why the temperature inside a closed car can rise to over 50°C. How can people prevent temperature increases in parked cars?

8 Electricity and Magnetism

STATIC ELECTRICITY
(pp. 152–154)

1. Name two types of electricity.
2. Explain what causes your hair to rise when you pull off a sweater.

Thinking like a Scientist
People often report a shock when touching a metal doorknob. Think of as many ways as you can to eliminate or reduce this static electricity. Design a doorknob that would be unlikely to cause this effect.

CURRENT ELECTRICITY
(pp. 155–157)

1. Name the lettered parts of the circuit in the drawing, using the terms *source of electricity, path, switch,* and *user of electricity.*

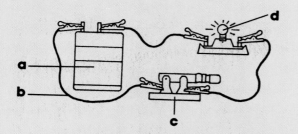

2. What would you call the circuit when the switch is open?

Thinking like a Scientist
A fuse is a device that helps solve an electrical problem. It is a strip of metal that can be placed into an electric circuit. When too much electricity passes through the strip, it gets hot and melts. This breaks the circuit. What problem does a fuse help solve?

MAKING ELECTRICITY
(pp. 158–159)

1. Describe how a flashlight battery makes electricity.
2. What is a generator?

Thinking like a Scientist
Large generators have a special part called a turbine. A turbine must move or spin before a generator can make electricity. The turbine in the drawing on page 159 is turned by moving water. Name two other sources of power that could be used to turn the turbine.

MAGNETISM

(pp. 160–163)

1. Describe a way the magnetic field of a magnet can be seen.
2. In what way are the two poles of a magnet different?
3. What is the difference between a normal piece of iron and a piece of iron that is a magnet?
4. These two poles are repelling each other. Identify poles 1, 2, and 3.

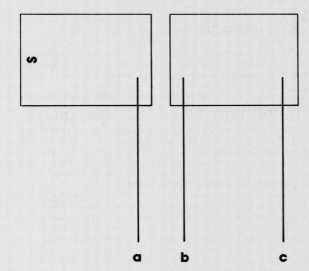

Thinking like a Scientist

The earth is a giant magnet. Make a drawing of the earth. Label each of the poles. Draw lines of force to show a magnetic field.

ELECTRICITY AND MAGNETISM

(pp. 164–165)

1. In what way can magnetism be used to produce electricity?
2. How can electricity be used to produce a magnet?

Thinking like a Scientist

The picture on page 164 shows an electromagnet being used in a scrapyard. Why do you think an electromagnet is used instead of a regular magnet?

9 Rocks and Minerals

INSIDE THE EARTH
(pp. 176–177)

1. Name the three layers of the earth shown here.

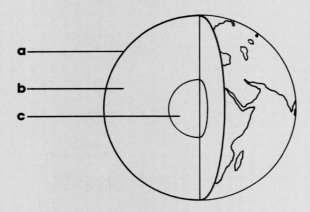

2. How is the crust of the earth different from the mantle?

Thinking like a Scientist
Suppose that you were going to try to drill through the earth's crust to reach the mantle. Where would you begin to drill? Why?

MINERALS
(pp. 178–180)

1. What do the particles that make up minerals join to form?

2. List a special property of a mineral and give an example of a mineral with that property.
3. Describe how scientists test the hardness of a mineral.

Thinking like a Scientist
Many phonograph needles are made of low-quality diamonds. Why would diamonds be the best material for this use?

MELTED ROCK
(pp. 181–184)

1. What is an igneous rock?
2. What is the difference between the way a mineral like granite forms and the way a mineral like obsidian forms?

Thinking like a Scientist
Pretend you have just landed on the moon. You begin to explore the surface. You suspect volcanoes at one time erupted on the surface near your spaceship. You collect rocks and return to your spaceship. How could you tell if the rocks you collected were formed by rapid or slow cooling of magma?

ROCKS FROM SEDIMENT
(pp. 185–187)

1. What is a sedimentary rock?
2. How is water important in forming many sedimentary rocks?

Thinking like a Scientist
Astronauts brought back many rocks from the moon's surface. Would you expect to find sedimentary rocks in the collection? Why or why not?

PLANTS AND ANIMALS FROM LONG AGO
(pp. 188–191)

1. What are fossils?
2. Tell whether each of the drawings shows a mold fossil or a cast fossil.

A   **B**   **C**

3. Name three fossil fuels. Tell how each is used.

Thinking like a Scientist
Pretend that you are talking to a person who does not know what fossil fuels are. How would you describe the formation of these fuels? How would you explain why it is so important to use fossil fuels wisely?

ROCKS THAT CHANGE INTO OTHER ROCKS
(pp. 192–193)

1. What is a metamorphic rock?
2. How is the metamorphic rock called hard coal different from the sedimentary rock called soft coal?

Thinking like a Scientist
Imagine that you are a famous artist. You have been hired to make a large statue for a new park. You can make your statue from marble or limestone. Which material would you use? Give reasons for your choice.

10   The Earth's Oceans

A LOOK AT THE OCEANS
(pp. 198–199)

1. How did the oceans become salty?
2. What is *Alvin*?

Thinking like a Scientist
A line from a poem says "Water, water everywhere, but not a drop to drink." What do you think the poet is describing?

THE OCEAN FLOOR
(pp. 200–203)

1. Describe the ocean floor, beginning with one continent and ending with the next continent.
2. How did the Hawaiian Islands form?

Thinking like a Scientist
What kind of living things would you expect to find in an ocean trench?

THE MOVING OCEAN
(pp. 204–208)

1. Explain why breakers occur near shore.
2. Identify where high tide and low tide would occur on the following drawing.

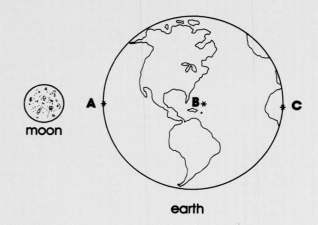

moon

earth

Thinking like a Scientist
People often speak of undertows along the ocean shore. What do you think an undertow is, and what do you think causes it?

THE OCEAN'S RIVERS
(pp. 209–211)

1. What are currents?
2. What is the Gulf Stream?
3. Identify the warm-water and cold-water currents in the following drawing. Write the letters *A* through *H* on a piece of paper. Write *cold* next to the letters that show cold-water currents. Write *warm* next to the letters that show warm-water currents.

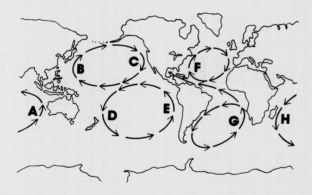

Thinking like a Scientist
During the early days of exploring the world, knowledge of ocean currents was important. Give a reason why this was true.

OCEAN RESOURCES
(pp. 212–214)

1. What is a resource?
2. What are nodules?
3. Name three products that can be made from seaweed.
4. What is tidal power? How is it being used?

Thinking like a Scientist
You have learned that the ocean bottom contains valuable minerals. What are some of the problems involved with using these minerals?

11 Measuring Weather

WEATHER AROUND US
(pp. 220–222)

1. What is the atmosphere?
2. Use the letters in the drawing to answer the following.

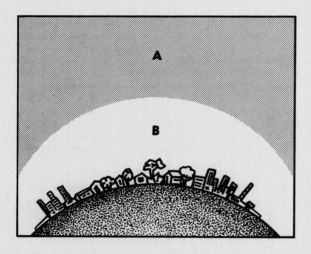

a. Which area is the troposphere?
b. In which area are the particles far apart?
c. In which area would a jet normally fly?

Thinking like a Scientist
A balloon filled with air at the earth's surface would expand and burst in the upper atmosphere. Why would this happen?

CHANGES IN AIR TEMPERATURE
(pp. 223–225)

1. How does heat from the sun cause weather changes on earth?
2. Would water at 20°C feel like it was hot, cold, or at room temperature?

Thinking like a Scientist
You have learned that the liquid part of the thermometer is colored alcohol. Why is alcohol used in thermometers instead of water?

AIR PRESSURE
(pp. 226–229)

1. Describe the air pressure in an area where warm air is rising.
2. Describe how a mercury barometer works.

Thinking like a Scientist
Use the information you learned in this lesson to explain how a hot-air balloon works. What makes the balloon rise? What does the person in the balloon have to do to bring it down to the ground?

WIND SPEED AND DIRECTION

(pp. 230–233)

1. Describe how differences in temperature help to produce wind.
2. Name the wind direction indicated by each of these weather vanes.

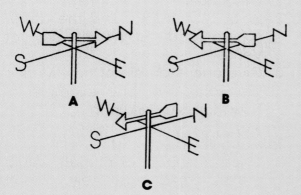

A

B

C

3. What is the Beaufort scale?

Thinking like a Scientist

How could you determine the wind direction without a weather vane? Describe at least three ways.

WATER IN THE AIR

(pp. 234–237)

1. How does water vapor eventually become precipitation?
2. Describe what a humid day is like.

Thinking like a Scientist

Sweat evaporating from your skin cools your body. On a humid day you feel warmer because sweat does not evaporate as quickly. Explain why.

12 The Solar System

THE SUN AND ITS FAMILY
(pp. 242–245)

1. Which of the drawings shows a planet rotating?

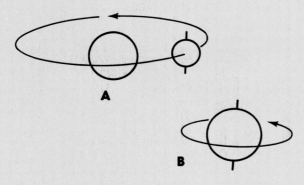

A

B

2. Which of the drawings shows a planet revolving?
3. What is the time it takes a planet to rotate once called? How long is this time on Earth?
4. Name the inner planets.

Thinking like a Scientist
How would Earth be different if it did not rotate on its axis?

THE INNER PLANETS
(pp. 246–250)

1. What is the fastest moving planet? Describe it.
2. What is unusual about the atmosphere and length of day of Venus?
3. Give one example of how Mars is like Earth and one example of how Mars is unlike Earth.

Thinking like a Scientist
Which of the inner planets would you think could most likely support life? Give reasons for your answer.

THE OUTER PLANETS

(pp. 251–256)

1. How are Jupiter and Saturn similar?
2. What is the Great Red Spot?
3. What is unusual about the way Uranus rotates?
4. What is unusual about the moons of Neptune?
5. Why will Pluto be the eighth planet until 1999?

Thinking like a Scientist

Look at the table on page 255. What can you say about the relationship of planet size and day length? How does the speed of Jupiter's rotation compare to Earth's? How does the distance of these planets from the sun compare with their size?

OTHER MEMBERS OF THE SOLAR SYSTEM

(pp. 257–259)

1. Identify and describe the objects labeled in the drawing.

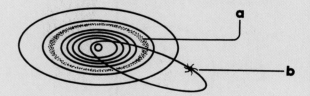

2. How is an asteroid different from a meteor?

Thinking like a Scientist

Pieces of rock such as meteors float through space for millions of years without changing. Yet when they enter our atmosphere, they burn up. Why does this happen?

13 Using Food

FROM CELLS TO SYSTEMS
(pp. 270–273)

1. What is a cell?
2. Name two kinds of cells.
3. Name and describe the body system shown in the picture.

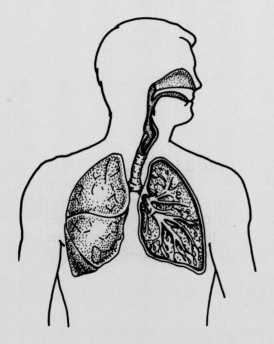

Thinking like a Scientist
Scientists use models to help them explain how things work. How are the cells of the human body like a factory and the workers in the factory?

USING WHAT YOU EAT
(pp. 274–275)

1. Give three reasons why food is important.
2. Describe the four basic steps of digestion.

Thinking like a Scientist
People who are sick or recovering from operations are given only liquids and soft foods to eat. Why do you think they are given these kinds of food?

DIGESTION IN THE MOUTH
(pp. 276–279)

1. Name each type of tooth in the drawing and explain its role in digestion.

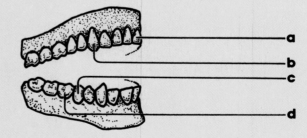

2. How does saliva help with digestion?

Write the name of an important type of tooth or teeth used in eating each of the foods below. Which foods could be eaten without teeth?

raw carrots   applesauce
steak   french fries
gelatin   hot dog
popcorn   apple

THE DIGESTIVE PATH
(pp. 280–284)

1. What is the esophagus?
2. Describe what the stomach does during digestion.
3. Name the parts of the digestive system in the drawing.

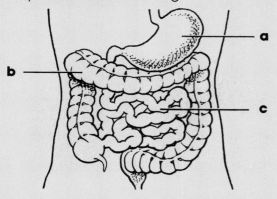

Thinking like a Scientist

Imagine the food you eat is digested in the stomach and passed to the small intestine. Here the food is further digested. What would happen if the digested food could not enter the bloodstream?

DIGESTIVE SYSTEM PROBLEMS
(pp. 285–286)

1. Why isn't it a good idea to do strenuous exercise immediately after eating a big meal?
2. Why are certain foods such as fruits and vegetables good for digestion?
3. What kind of problem can occur as a result of eating too many spicy foods?

Thinking like a Scientist

Long-distance runners will eat large amounts of high-energy foods for several days before a big race. Then for several hours before the race, they will not eat. Why do you think they do this?

14 The Sense Organs

SENSE ORGANS AND THE BRAIN
(pp. 292–294)

1. Name the five senses.
2. Name the five sense organs.

Thinking like a Scientist

Scientists use models to help them explain how things work. How is the human brain like a library and a telephone switchboard?

THE EYE AND SIGHT
(pp. 295–298)

1. Identify the lens, retina, and nerve in this drawing.

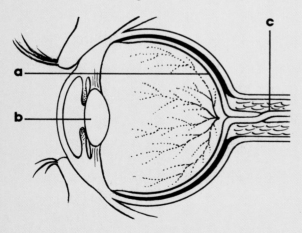

2. Describe how the eye works.

Thinking like a Scientist

The small opening through which light enters the eye can change its size. Which drawing shows the eye in bright light? Which one shows the eye in darkness? Give a reason for your choices.

A   B

THE EARS AND HEARING
(pp. 299–301)

1. Identify the ear canal, middle ear, inner ear, eardrum, and outer ear in this drawing.

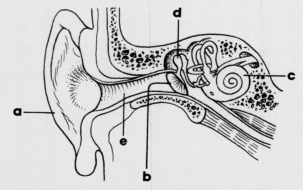

2. Describe good ear care.

Thinking like a Scientist

Look at the pictures below. Describe how hearing is changed in each one. Explain your answer.

THE TONGUE AND THE NOSE
(pp. 302–304)

1. What four tastes can the tongue detect?
2. Which of the four tastes could you first detect in foods?
3. Why must you sniff a flower in order to smell it?

Thinking like a Scientist

Explain why people who have colds cannot taste the food they eat.

THE SKIN
(pp. 305–308)

1. Identify the epidermis, dermis, nerve endings, and hairs in this drawing.

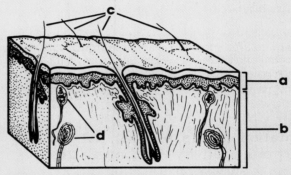

2. Why is feeling pain important?
3. Describe important steps for skin care.

Thinking like a Scientist

Some parts of your body are more sensitive to touch than others. Pinch the skin over your elbow. Do you feel sharp pain? Explain the differences in sense of touch for different parts of the body.

GLOSSARY

Key to Pronunciation
a apple, bat	**i** if, pig	**sh** she, wish	**ə** stands for:
ā ate, page	**ī** idea, fine	**th** think, moth	a in asleep
ã air, care	**ng** ring, sink	**ŦH** the, bathe	e in garden
ä father, star	**o** ox, top	**u** uncle, sun	i in pencil
ch chest, such	**ō** owe, no	**ù** pull, foot	o in button
e egg, bed	**ô** orbit, saw	**ü** glue, boot	u in circus
ē even, me	**oi** oil, joy	**zh** usual, vision	
ėr earn, bird	**ou** out, mouse		

This Key to Pronunciation is adapted from *Scott, Foresman Intermediate Dictionary,* by E. L. Thorndike and Clarence L. Barnhart. Copyright © 1983 by Scott, Foresman and Company. Reprinted by permission.

adaptation (ad ap tā′shən) A body part or an activity that helps a living thing to survive. *p. 67*

air pressure The downward push of the air in the atmosphere. *p. 226*

algae A group of nonseed plants that do not have true roots, stems, or leaves. *p. 37*

anemometer (an ə mom′ə tər) An instrument used to measure wind speed. *p. 232*

animal population (pop yə lā′shən) A group of the same kind of animal living in an area. *p. 4*

asteroid (as′tə roid) A piece of rock that orbits the sun between Mars and Jupiter. *p. 258*

atmosphere (at′mə sfir) The air that surrounds the earth. *p. 222*

balance A tool for measuring mass. *p. 100*

barometer (bə rom′ə tər) An instrument used to measure changes in air pressure. *p. 228*

battery An object that changes chemical energy into electricity. *p. 158*

breaker A wave that falls as it comes close to shore. *p. 205*

calorie (kal′ər ē) A unit used to measure heat energy. *p. 135*

canines (kā′nīns) The pointed teeth next to the incisors. *p. 276*

carnivore (kär′nə vôr)   An animal that eats only other animals. *p. 51*

cast fossil   A rock with the exact shape of a plant or animal from long ago. *p. 189*

cell   The smallest part of the body. *p. 270*

centimeter (sen′tə mē tər)   A unit used to measure length. *p. 96*

circuit (ser′kit)   The path along which negative charges flow. *p. 155*

comet (kom′it)   A mass of frozen gas and dust orbiting the sun. *p. 257*

community (kə myü′nə tē)   All the plants and animals that live in an area. *p. 59*

complete circuit   A circuit whose path is not broken. *p. 156*

compound machine   A machine made of two or more simple machines. *p. 126*

conduction (kən duk′shən)   The movement of heat energy through a solid. *p. 140*

conductor (kən duk′tər)   Any material through which energy moves easily. *p. 141*

conifer (kō′nə fər)   A seed plant that has cones. *p. 33*

consumer (kən sü′mər)   A name given to animals, because they must eat food to get energy. *p. 49*

continental (kon tə nen′təl) **shelf**   The underwater edge of a continent. *p. 200*

continental slope   A steep drop in the ocean floor after the continental shelf. *p. 201*

convection (kən vek′shən)   The movement of heat energy through a liquid or a gas. *p. 143*

core   The inner layer of the earth. *p. 176*

crest   The top part of a wave. *p. 205*

crust   An outer layer of rock that covers the whole earth. *p. 176*

current (ker′ənt)   A large moving river of water in an ocean. *p. 209*

current electricity   A kind of electricity produced when negative charges flow along a path. *p. 155*

degree Celsius (di grē′ sel′sē əs)   A unit used to measure temperature. *p. 137*

density (den′sə tē)   The mass in a certain volume. *p. 107*

dermis (dèr′mis)   The inner layer of the skin. *p. 306*

dicot (dī′kot)   A plant whose seeds have two sections. *p. 30*

digestive system   The system used to break down food in the body. *p. 275*

drone   A male bee in a honeybee colony. *p. 11*

dry cell battery   A battery made of a zinc case, a carbon rod, and a chemical paste. *p. 158*

ear canal   The part of the ear between the outer ear and the eardrum. *p. 300*

eardrum   A thin tissue at the end of the ear canal. *p. 300*

Earth   The third planet from the sun. *p. 248*

energy   The ability to do work. *p. 114*

epidermis (ep ə dėr′mis)   The top layer of the skin. *p. 306*

esophagus (ē sof′ə gəs)   A tube that carries food to the stomach. *p. 280*

ferns   A group of nonseed plants that have roots, stems, and leaves. *p. 36*

food chain   The path by which energy passes from one living thing to another. *p. 55*

food web   Something that shows how all the animals in a community get energy. *p. 59*

fossil (fos′əl)   A trace of a plant or animal found in a sedimentary rock. *p. 180*

friction (frik′shən)   A force that slows down or stops motion. *p. 125*

fungi   A group of nonseed plants that cannot make their own food. *p. 37*

generator (jen′ə rā tər)   A machine that uses a magnet to make electricity. *p. 159*

graduate (graj′ü it)   A tool used to measure the volume of liquids. *p. 104*

gram   A unit used to measure mass. *p. 101*

herbivore (her′bə vôr)   An animal that eats only plants. *p. 50*

herd   A group of animals that live together, such as cattle, elephants, and whales. *p. 16*

hiberation (hī bər nā′shən)   A long period of deep sleep used by some animals to survive the winter. *p. 83*

high tide   The rise in the level of ocean water. *p. 207*

high-pressure area   An area of cool sinking air. *p. 227*

host   A living thing that a parasite depends on. *p. 19*

humidity (hyü mid′ə tē)   Water in the air. *p. 236*

hygrometer (hī grom′ə tər)   An instrument used to measure humidity. *p. 237*

igneous (ig′nē əs) **rock**   A kind of rock formed from magma. *p. 181*

incisors (in sī′zərs)   The teeth in the front of your mouth. *p. 276*

inclined plane   A simple machine made of a slanted surface. *p. 123*

incomplete circuit   A circuit whose path is broken. *p. 156*

inner ear   The part of the ear shaped like a long coiled tube. *p. 300*

inner planets   The four planets closest to the sun. *p. 244*

insect colony (kol′ə nē)   A group of insects that live together. *p. 9*

insulator (in′sə lā tər)   Any material through which energy does not move easily. *p. 141*

Jupiter (jü′pə tər)   The fifth planet from the sun. *p. 251*

kilogram (kil′ə gram)   A unit of mass equal to 1,000 g. *p. 101*

kilometer (kil′ə mē tər)   A unit of length equal to 1,000 m. *p. 98*

kinetic (ki net′ik) **energy**   The energy of motion. *p. 117*

large intestine   A short tube through which water removed from food enters the body. *p. 282*

length   A measured distance. *p. 96*

lens   Part of the eye that bends light onto the retina. *p. 296*

lever   A simple machine made of a bar or rod that turns on a point. *p. 120*

liter   A unit of volume equal to 1,000 mL. *p. 105*

low tide   The fall in the level of ocean water. *p. 207*

low–pressure area   An area of warm rising air. *p. 227*

magnet   An object that attracts metals such as iron and steel. *p. 160*

magnetic field   The space around a magnet in which a magnetic force can be found. *p. 160*

mantle (man′təl)   The middle layer of the earth. *p. 176*

Mars   The fourth planet from the sun. *p. 249*

mass   The amount of matter in an object. *p. 99*

matter   Anything that has mass and takes up space. *p. 94*

Mercury (mėr'kyər ē)   The planet closest to the sun. *p. 246*

metamorphic (met ə môr'fik) **rock**   A kind of rock formed when other kinds of rocks are changed by great heat and pressure. *p. 192*

meteor (mē'tē ər)   A rock from space that has been pulled into the earth's atmosphere. *p. 259*

meteorite (mē'tē ə rīt)   A meteor that strikes the ground. *p. 259*

meter   A unit of length equal to 100 cm. *p. 98*

middle ear   The part of the ear made up of three small bones. *p. 300*

migration (mī grā'shən)   An adaptation of traveling great distances to survive the winter. *p. 80*

milliliter (mil'ə lē tər)   A unit used to measure the volume of liquids. *p. 104*

mineral (min'ər əl)   A pure, solid material found in the earth's crust. *p. 178*

molars (mō'lərs)   The teeth with large flat tops found at the back of the mouth. *p. 277*

mold fossil   An empty space in a sedimentary rock where a plant or animal used to be. *p. 188*

monocot (mon'ə kot)   A plant whose seeds have one section. *p. 30*

moss   A kind of nonseed plant that does not have true roots, stems, or leaves. *p. 37*

Neptune (nep'tün)   The eighth planet from the sun. *p. 253*

nodule (noj'ül)   A rock, which contains minerals, that is found on the ocean floor. *p. 213*

omnivore (om'nə vôr)   An animal that eats both plants and other animals. *p. 52*

organ (ôr'gən)   A group of tissues that works together in the body. *p. 272*

outer ear   The part of the ear outside the head. *p. 300*

outer planets   The five planets farthest from the sun. *p. 244*

parasite (par'ə sīt)   A living thing that depends on and harms other living things. *p. 19*

plain   The bottom of the ocean floor. *p. 202*

Pluto (plü'tō)   The most distant planet from the sun. *p. 253*

pole   The end of a magnet. *p. 161*

potential (pə ten'shel) **energy**   Stored energy. *p. 118*

prairie (prãr′ē) **dog town**   An area where prairie dogs live. *p. 5*

precipitation (pri sip ə tā′shən) Water from the atmosphere that falls to the ground. *p. 234*

premolars (prē mō′lərs)   The teeth with flat tops that are found between the canines and the molars. *p. 277*

producer (prə dü′sər)   A name given to green plants, because they can make their own food. *p. 48*

property (prop′ər tē)   Something that describes matter. *p. 95*

pulley   A simple machine made of a grooved wheel and a rope, chain, or belt. *p. 124*

queen   The bee that lays all the eggs in a honeybee colony. *p. 11*

radiation (rā dē ā′shən)   The movement of heat energy in waves. *p. 145*

resource (ri sôrs′)   A useful material taken from the earth. *p. 212*

retina   The back wall of the eye. *p. 296*

saliva (sə lī′və)   A juice released in the mouth. *p. 278*

Saturn (sat′ərn)   The sixth planet from the sun. *p. 252*

school   A group of the same kind of fish that live together. *p. 13*

sedimentary (sed ə men′tər ē) **rock**   A rock formed from sediment. *p. 186*

sense organs   The parts of the body used for seeing, hearing, tasting, smelling, and touching. *p. 292*

simple machine   A machine made of very few parts. *p. 120*

small intestine (in tes′tən)   A long tube in the digestive system. Most of the food used by the body enters the bloodstream through the small intestine. *p. 281*

spores   The cells in nonseed plants used to reproduce. *p. 36*

static electricity   A kind of electricity made by friction. *p. 152*

stomach   A hollow organ that mixes food with digestive juices. *p. 280*

system   A group of cells, tissues, and organs that works together in the body. *p. 273*

taste buds   The cells in the tongue used for tasting. *p. 302*

temperature (tem′pər ə chər)   A measure of how hot or cold matter is. *p. 136*

tendril (ten′drəl)   A thin coiled structure that helps a plant to climb. *p. 71*

tide   A change in the level of ocean water. *p. 206*

tissue (tish´ü)   A group of cells that works together to do certain jobs in the body. *p. 271*

tongue   An organ in the mouth that is part of the digestive system. *p. 278*

trench   A deep, narrow slit in the ocean floor. *p. 203*

trough (trôf)   The bottom part of a wave. *p. 205*

Uranus (yur´ə nəs)   The seventh planet from the sun. *p. 253*

Venus (vē´nəs)   The second planet from the sun. *p. 247*

volume (vol´yəm)   The amount of space an object takes up. *p. 103*

water vapor   Water as a gas. *p. 234*

weather   The condition of the air around us. *p. 220*

wet cell battery   A battery made of lead, water, and acid. *p. 159*

wheel and axle   A simple machine made of a wheel connected to an axle. *p. 123*

worker   A female bee that does most of the jobs in a honeybee colony. *p. 11*

INDEX

CREDITS

1 2 3 4 5 6 7 8 9 10—VH—90 89 88 87 86 85 84